TEACHER GUIDE

Includes Stud
Worksheet

10th–12th Grade

Languag
Studies

Answer Key

Intro to Biblical Greek

First printing: June 2017
Second printing: April 2019

Copyright © 2017 by Master Books®. All rights reserved. No part of this book may be used or reproduced in any manner whatsoever without written permission of the publisher, except in the case of brief quotations in articles and reviews.

For information write:

Master Books®, P.O. Box 726, Green Forest, AR 72638

Master Books® is a division of the New Leaf Publishing Group, Inc.

ISBN: 978-1-68344-100-7
ISBN: 978-1-61458-618-0 (digital)

Unless otherwise noted, Scripture quotations are from the New King James Version of the Bible.

Printed in the United States of America

Please visit our website for other great titles:
www.masterbooks.com

For information regarding author interviews,
please contact the publicity department at (870) 438-5288.

Permission is granted for copies of reproducible pages from this text to be made for use within your own homeschooling family activities. Material may not be posted online, distributed digitally, or made available as a download. Permission for any other use of the material must be requested prior to use by email to the publisher at info@nlpg.com.

Your reputation as a publisher is stellar. It is a blessing knowing anything I purchase from you is going to be worth every penny!

—Cheri ★★★★★

Last year we found Master Books and it has made a HUGE difference.

—Melanie ★★★★★

We love Master Books and the way it's set up for easy planning!

—Melissa ★★★★★

You have done a great job. MASTER BOOKS ROCKS!

—Stephanie ★★★★★

Physically high-quality, Biblically faithful, and well-written.

—Danika ★★★★★

Best books ever. Their illustrations are captivating and content amazing!

—Kathy ★★★★★

Affordable
Flexible
Faith Building

Table of Contents

Author Bio:
Todd Friel is a fun and engaging speaker with a knack for making things like Greek and hermeneutics easy to understand. His presentations are filled with a mix of humor and a strong Biblical foundation. He is the host of the nationally syndicated Wretched TV and Wretched Radio programs, and author of *Jesus Unmasked, Stressed Out,* and *Reset for Parents.* He is also the author and producer of over two dozen Bible study courses. Todd has one wife, three children, and a dog.

Using This Teacher Guide

Features: The suggested weekly schedule enclosed has easy-to-manage lessons that guide the video program, worksheets, and all assessments. The pages of this guide are perforated and three-hole punched so materials are easy to tear out, hand out, grade, and store. Teachers are encouraged to adjust the schedule and materials needed in order to best work within their unique educational program.

Lesson Scheduling: Students are instructed to watch the lessons on their DVD and then complete the corresponding section provided by the teacher. Assessments that may include worksheets, activities, quizzes, and tests are given at regular intervals with space to record each grade. Space is provided on the weekly schedule for assignment dates, and flexibility in scheduling is encouraged. Teachers may adapt the scheduled days per each unique student situation. As the student completes each assignment, this can be marked with an "X" in the box.

Approximately 15 to 30 minutes per lesson, three to four days a week

Includes answer keys for worksheets, practice sheets, and quizzes

Worksheets for each video lesson

Quizzes are included to help reinforce learning and provide assessment opportunities.

Designed for grades 10 to 12 in a one-year course to earn ½ language credit

Course Objectives: Students completing this course will learn

- the Greek alphabet
- punctuation and how it is used
- nouns, verbs, voice, and moods
- nominative, genitives, vocatives, accusatives, and datives
- how to understand many of the Greek references your pastor makes
- the importance of properly translating the Bible
- how a concordance and lexicon work

Course Description

Intro to Biblical Greek is an elective course that lays the groundwork for further study of the language.

The purpose of the course is to simplify many of the basic concepts of biblical Greek and give you an edge should you continue with more advanced studies of the language. This is not structured as a typical language course. It is essentially a "starter kit" that will get you reading and understanding biblical Greek. It will not give you a daily lesson on pronunciation or practicing verb conjugation, but is instead designed to give you a working knowledge of biblical Greek, not a specific mastery of it.

This video-based learning program is a basic introduction to biblical or Koine Greek. Complete a flexible course that includes suggestions for lesson schedules depending on how extensive you want the course to be. Student worksheets, practice sheets, quizzes, answer keys, and suggested ongoing resources and projects to enhance learning are included in this teacher guide.

Developed for use by individuals or families, now in just one semester you can go beyond simple memorization to actually begin to grasp the meaning and message of the Greek texts! An understanding of biblical Greek can help students understand the truths of the New Testament in a deeper way, as well as grasp the fullness of God's perfect timing, using a vastly known language to communicate the Good News of Jesus Christ throughout the Western world. Be inspired to love the Savior more as you grasp the Bible's message more clearly!

The course consists of 10 lessons on DVD. Student and parent educators have flexibility in how they wish to use the schedule based on the abilities and interests of each individual learner. The course is flexible enough to be worked into an existing course schedule with little disruption. Advanced students could complete this course in a two-week period if lessons are limited only to the DVDs and memorization of the Greek alphabet — however, enough activities and course materials are included in the student worksheets to last a semester using the suggested daily schedule. Course expansion ideas for students wanting to take their study to a full year are also provided.

Course Expansion: As noted, the course can be a straightforward introduction of biblical Greek, limited to the scope of the DVD lessons, or the course can be expanded in any number of ways that would offer additional hours to earn additional course credit.

Use internet resources and websites to add additional material or practice opportunities (i.e., reading and writing opportunities). There are many great online resources. Here are a few to get you started:

www.ibiblio.org/koine/greek/lessons/

www.billmounce.com/classes

www.thebereanapproach.com/id9.html

Translation comparisons — choose 5 to 10 verses at the start of the course from no more than three biblical translations. Have the student write their understanding of each before the course begins. Once the DVD lessons are over, the student needs to write each verse in biblical Greek and write their understanding of it in this language. Then, those thoughts can be compared and contrasted with their thoughts on the other translations chosen for verses at the beginning of the course.

Term paper — topics could include how the use of biblical Greek helped to spread Christianity and the early church, how languages like Koine Greek evolve as a "street" language of the people, a comparison of Koine vs. Classical Greek, or what criteria serious Bible students can use to evaluate various commentaries.

Master the use of a lexicon — understand how and why it can be an effective tool for biblical study. Use a lexicon to translate a chapter or book of the Bible.

Google Books has a variety of free ebooks related to the study and understanding of biblical Greek. Reading assignments and other tasks could be based on any of these per the student's interest and desire to dig deeper into the language.

Grading Options for This Course: It is always the prerogative of an educator to assess student grades however he or she might deem best. The following is only a suggested guideline based on the material presented through this course:

To calculate the percentage of the worksheets and quizzes, the educator may use the following guide. Divide total number of questions correct (example: 43) by the total number of questions possible (example: 46) to calculate the percentage out of 100 possible. 43/46 = 93 percent correct.

The suggested grade values are noted as follows: 90 to 100 percent = A; 80 to 89 percent = B; 70 to 79 percent = C; 60 to 69 percent = D; and 0 to 59 percent = F.

Recommended Resources:

The Basics of Biblical Greek by Dr. William D. Mounce.

Interlinear Bible, *Strong's Concordance*, lexicon, commentaries (all of these can be found online for free at www.biblehub.com).

Also, another great resource for home Bible study would be a *Word Study Greek-English New Testament.*

Semester Suggested Daily Schedule

Date	Day	Assignment	Due Date	✓	Grade
		Semester-First Quarter			
Week 1	Day 1	**Watch Lesson 1** • *It's Not Greek to Me* DVD			
	Day 2	**Greek Lesson 1: Worksheet 1** • Pages 15-16 • Teacher Guide • (TG)			
	Day 3	**Greek Lesson 1: Worksheet 2** • Pages 17-18 • (TG)			
	Day 4				
	Day 5				
Week 2	Day 6	**Watch Lesson 2** • *It's Not Greek to Me* DVD			
	Day 7	**Greek Lesson 2: Worksheet 1** • Page 19 • (TG)			
	Day 8	**Greek Lesson 2: Worksheet 2** • Pages 21-22 • (TG)			
	Day 9				
	Day 10				
Week 3	Day 11	**Practice Sheet 1** • Page 65 • (TG)			
	Day 12	**Practice Sheet 2** • Page 67 • (TG)			
	Day 13	**Practice Sheet 3** • Page 69 • (TG)			
	Day 14	**Practice Sheet 4** • Page 71 • (TG)			
	Day 15				
Week 4	Day 16	**Greek Lesson 2: Worksheet 3** • Page 23 • (TG)			
	Day 17	**Practice Sheet 5** • Page 73 • (TG)			
	Day 18	**Greek Lesson 2: Worksheet 4** • Page 25 • (TG)			
	Day 19				
	Day 20				
Week 5	Day 21	**Watch Lesson 3** • *It's Not Greek to Me* DVD			
	Day 22	**Greek Lesson 3: Worksheet 1** • Page 27 • (TG)			
	Day 23	**Practice Sheet 6** • Page 75 • (TG)			
	Day 24	**Practice Sheet 7** • Page 77 • (TG)			
	Day 25				
Week 6	Day 26	**Greek Lesson 3: Worksheet 2** • Page 29 • (TG)			
	Day 27	**Greek Lesson 3: Worksheet 3** • Page 31 • (TG)			
	Day 28				
	Day 29	**Pre-Quiz Review Day, Lessons 1-3**			
	Day 30	**Quiz 1** • Lessons 1–3 • Pages 103-104 • (TG)			
Week 7	Day 31	**Watch Lesson 4** • *It's Not Greek to Me* DVD			
	Day 32	**Greek Lesson 4: Worksheet 1** • Page 33 • (TG)			
	Day 33	**Practice Sheet 8** • Page 79 • (TG)			
	Day 34	**Greek Lesson 4: Worksheet 2** • Pages 35-36 • (TG)			
	Day 35				

Date	Day	Assignment	Due Date	✓	Grade
Week 8	Day 36	**Practice Sheet 9** • Page 81 • (TG)			
	Day 37	**Greek Lesson 4: Worksheet 3** • Pages 37-38 • (TG)			
	Day 38	**Practice Sheet 10** • Page 83 • (TG)			
	Day 39				
	Day 40				
Week 9	Day 41	**Watch Lesson 5** • *It's Not Greek to Me* DVD			
	Day 42	**Greek Lesson 5: Worksheet 1** • Pages 39-40 • (TG)			
	Day 43	**Greek Lesson 5: Worksheet 2** • Page 41 • (TG)			
	Day 44				
	Day 45	**Pre-Quiz Review Day, Lessons 4–5**			
		Semester-Second Quarter			
Week 1	Day 46	**Quiz 2** • Lessons 4–5 • Pages 105-106 • (TG)			
	Day 47				
	Day 48	**Watch Lesson 6** • *It's Not Greek to Me* DVD			
	Day 49	**Greek Lesson 6: Worksheet 1** • Pages 43-44 • (TG)			
	Day 50	**Practice Sheet 11** • Pages 85-86 • (TG)			
Week 2	Day 51	**Greek Lesson 6: Worksheet 2** • Pages 45-46 • (TG)			
	Day 52	**Practice Sheet 12** • Pages 87-88 • (TG)			
	Day 53	**Watch Lesson 7** • *It's Not Greek to Me* DVD			
	Day 54	**Greek Lesson 7: Worksheet 1** • Page 47 • (TG)			
	Day 55				
Week 3	Day 56	**Practice Sheet 13** • Pages 89-90 • (TG)			
	Day 57	**Practice Sheet 14** • Pages 91-92 • (TG)			
	Day 58	**Greek Lesson 7: Worksheet 2** • Pages 49-50 • (TG)			
	Day 59	**Practice Sheet 15** • Pages 93-94 • (TG)			
	Day 60				
Week 4	Day 61	**Pre-Quiz Review Day, Lessons 6–7**			
	Day 62	**Quiz 3** • Lessons 6–7 • Pages 107-108 • (TG)			
	Day 63				
	Day 64	**Watch Lesson 8** • *It's Not Greek to Me* DVD			
	Day 65	**Greek Lesson 8: Worksheet 1** • Page 51 • (TG)			
Week 5	Day 66	**Greek Lesson 8: Worksheet 2** • Pages 53-54 • (TG)			
	Day 67	**Practice Sheet 16** • Page 95 • (TG)			
	Day 68	**Greek Lesson 8: Worksheet 3** • Pages 55-56 • (TG)			
	Day 69				
	Day 70				

Date	Day	Assignment	Due Date	✓	Grade
Week 6	Day 71	**Watch Lesson 9** • *It's Not Greek to Me* DVD			
	Day 72	**Greek Lesson 9: Worksheet 1** • Pages 57-58 • (TG)			
	Day 73				
	Day 74	**Greek Lesson 9: Worksheet 2** • Pages 59-60 • (TG)			
	Day 75	**Practice Sheet 17** • Pages 97-98 • (TG)			
Week 7	Day 76	**Practice Sheet 18** • Pages 99-100 • (TG)			
	Day 77				
	Day 78	**Watch Lesson 10** • *It's Not Greek to Me* DVD			
	Day 79	**Greek Lesson 10: Worksheet 1** • Pages 61-62 • (TG)			
	Day 80				
Week 8	Day 81	**Pre-Quiz Review Day, Lessons 8–10**			
	Day 82	**Quiz 4** • Lessons 8–10 • Pages 109-110 • (TG)			
	Day 83				
	Day 84	**Review Lessons 1–3: *It's Not Greek to Me* DVD**			
	Day 85				
Week 9	Day 86	**Review Lessons 4–5: *It's Not Greek to Me* DVD**			
	Day 87				
	Day 88	**Review Lessons 6–7: *It's Not Greek to Me* DVD**			
	Day 89				
	Day 90	**Review Lessons 8–10: *It's Not Greek to Me* DVD**			
		Final Grade			

Greek Alphabet Chart

Case		English Name	Transliteration
Upper	Lower		
Α	α	alpha	a
Β	β	beta	b
Γ	γ	gamma	g[1]
Δ	δ	delta	d
Ε	ε	epsilon	e
Ζ	ζ	zeta	z
Η	η	eta	ê or e
Θ	θ	theta	th
Ι	ι	iota	i
Κ	κ	kappa	k
Λ	λ	lambda	l
Μ	μ	mu	m
Ν	ν	nu	n
Ξ	ξ	xi	x
Ο	ο	omicron	o
Π	π	pi	p
Ρ	ρ	rho	r
Σ	ς or σ	sigma	s
Τ	τ	tau	t
Υ	υ	upsilon	u or y
Φ	φ	phi	ph
Χ	χ	chi	ch
Ψ	ψ	psi	ps
Ω	ω	omega	ô or o

1. Gamma. When gamma is found in combination with another consonant, it may be transliterated as an "n"; γγ = ng; γκ = nk; γξ = nx; γχ = nch (gutenberg.org/wiki/Gutenberg:Greek_How-To). Follow the gutenberg.org link for additional information on transliteration.

What is transliteration?

When you write letters from one alphabet into corresponding letters from another alphabet, it is called transliteration. It is an important concept to know because often it is used rather than the original alphabet of the language for easier understanding.

What about pronunciations?

If you are interested in learning more about pronunciation of biblical Greek, the following link explains some of the challenges and pronunciations that you can explore: www.biblicalgreek.org/grammar/pronunciation

Greek Language Worksheets

for Use with

It's Not Greek to Me

DVD Learning Program

Welcome to "It's Not Greek to Me: Knowing Enough to Be Dangerous."

Your teacher has an inferiority complex and prefers to be called Mr. ________________.

This course is for you if:

1. You are a layperson who wants to ________________________________.

2. You plan on studying ____________________ Greek.

What you will not learn:

1. How to ______________________.

To translate means what?

To interpret means what?

2. Vocables = ____________________.

3. Endings

Activity

Look up the word "declension." What does it mean? Does the dictionary you used have an example? If so, write it down.

What you will learn:

1. How to ______________ Greek.

2. How to ___________________ Greek.

3. How the language works. Nike says, "Just Do It!" We say, "Just _________ It!"

4. How to utilize a _________________________.

5. How to use a __________________________.

6. Your English will get "gooder" (or more correctly ________________)!

7. You will recognize Greek roots in many English words:
   >Ergon = _________________.

   >Adelphos = _______________.

8. Can check the Scriptures yourself to discern true from _____________ teaching.

9. Get more out of ____________________________.

10. Understand your _________________ when he makes Greek language references.

11. You will see the brilliance of God in using the Greek language to get the Good News to all nations. Classical Greek: 8th to 4th century B.C. and during the time of Homer to Plato. It was very precise and nuanced, far more than Hebrew, and far less messy. In the fourth century, Phillip of Macedonia conquered Athens. His son, Alexander the Great, studied under Aristotle and learned Greek. It was Alexander's desire to Hellenize the world and the Greek language was a part of it. But this sophisticated language soon started getting mingled with other languages and the result was Koine = street (or common) Greek. This is the language the New Testament was written in. **Give an example of a word from a language other than English that has been widely adopted.**

    Why did God choose this language? Give three examples. Why was this important?

12. You will love your ______________________ more.

    Study the following example. Take a ruler or piece of paper and cover all but the top line. Then reveal the second, then the third.

John 1:1

ἐν	ἀρχῇ	ἦν	ὁ	λόγος	καὶ	ὁ	λόγος	ἦν	πρὸς	τὸν	θεόν
en	archē	ēn	o	logos	kai	o	logos	ēn	pros	ton	theon
In	beginning	was	the	word	and	the	word	was	with	the	God

It is important to understand how letters form the words that form the text in both Greek and English.

Special Activity

Read Philippians 2:5–11, then note your first impressions of the text and what you believe was meant by Paul when he first wrote this to the church at Philippi. You will read this same passage at the end of the course in Lesson Ten with your new tools for understanding Scripture!

Bad news: not everyone pronounces Koine Greek the same way.

Good news: You can goof and blame it on your teacher.

We get the word *alphabet* from the first two letters in Greek: ________ ________.

Greek used to be written with all capital letters. Now, capital letters are only used in proper names, cities/states, and at the beginning of a sentence.

There are 24 letters in the Greek alphabet and you need to memorize them. You must be able to recognize, pronounce, and write the letters. **On page 11 of the study guide, there is a removable alphabet chart to assist you with this.** In addition, you will find an excellent online memorization resource for learning the alphabet at http://memorize.com/greek-alphabet. For pronunciation practice, please review the video.

Part 1: Alpha – MU

Memorize Alpha – Mu. When you become proficient in recognizing, pronouncing, and writing the letters move on to Part 2.

Case		English Name
Upper	Lower	
Α	α	alpha
Β	β	beta
Γ	γ	gamma
Δ	δ	delta
Ε	ε	epsilon
Ζ	ζ	zeta
Η	η	eta
Θ	θ	theta
Ι	ι	iota
Κ	κ	kappa
Λ	λ	lambda
Μ	μ	mu

Part 2: Nu – Omega

Memorize Nu – Omega. When you become proficient in recognizing, pronouncing, and writing the letters, move on to Part 3 on Lesson 2, Worksheet 2.

Case		English Name
Upper	Lower	
Ν	ν	nu
Ξ	ξ	xi
Ο	ο	omicron
Π	π	pi
Ρ	ρ	rho
Σ	ς or σ	sigma
Τ	τ	tau
Υ	υ	upsilon
Φ	φ	phi
Χ	χ	chi
Ψ	ψ	psi
Ω	ω	omega

Part 3: Vowels and Dipthongs

Memorize the Greek vowels and dipthongs. You want to be able to recognize, pronounce, and write them from memory.

There are seven vowels in the Greek alphabet, and they will have either a long or short sound.

Greek Vowels	
Short	Long
α (alpha) – as in father	α (alpha) – same only held longer
ε (epsilon) – as in sled	η (eta) – as in play
ο (omicron) – as in Ontario	ω (omega) – as in boat
ι (iota) – as in fish	ι (iota) – as in police
υ (upsilon) – as in flute	υ (upsilon) – same only held longer

Four of the vowels are considered "open" and three are "closed." Say "a" as in adoption and you will notice your throat feels open. Say the letter "i" as in dipstick and you will notice your throat feels closed or constricted.

The **open vowels** are α, ε, η, ο, ω.

The **closed vowels** are ι, υ.

Vowel combinations are called dipthongs. Dipthongs are two vowels combined to make one new sound.

> There are no silent letters in Greek pronunciation. Every letter sound is pronounced except vowel combinations (dipthongs). It is important to memorize the dipthongs because not every vowel combination is a dipthong. Sometimes you have to pronounce the two vowels separately.

Example: οι is a dipthong, but ιο is not. (Compare the ***oi* in Illinois** with the ***io* in Ohio**. The ***oi*** in Illin**ois** makes one vowel sound, whereas the ***i*** and ***o*** in Oh**io** are clearly two distinct sounds).

Proper Greek Dipthongs

αι is pronounced ai	as in Thailand or aisle
ει is pronounced ei	as in eight or freight
οι is pronounced oi	as in Illinois or oil
αυ is pronounced ow	as in cow or bow
ευ is pronounced eu	as in feud or fuel
ηυ is pronounced the same as ευ	as in feud or fuel
ου is pronounced ou	as in soup or food
υι is pronounced uee	as in queen

Improper Greek dipthongs are: ᾳ, ῃ, and ῳ. These improper dipthongs contain an iota subscript that serves as the second vowel. What is an ι (iota) subscript? When a small ι appears underneath either one of these letters, it is called an improper dipthong or iota subscript (because it is UNDER a letter). While the ι is not pronounced, it can change the meaning of the word, so it should not be ignored.

Do NOT move forward until you have your alphabet and diphthongs memorized! There will be a quiz. No, I am not kidding. You have to learn this. Don't make me turn this lesson around!

Greek Alphabet Quiz

Fill in the following table with the Greek alphabet. (The upper case letters are for bonus points.)

Upper Case	Lower Case	English Name

Greek Dipthong Quiz

1. List all seven proper dipthongs.
    1.
    2.
    3.
    4.
    5.
    6.
    7.

2. List all three improper dipthongs.
    1.
    2.
    3.

3. List all seven vowels.
    1.
    2.
    3.
    4.
    5.
    6.
    7.

4. Which vowels are open?

There are five Greek punctuation marks:

, (looks like an English comma) = __________

. (looks like an English period) = __________

• (looks like a high period) = ______________

: (looks like an English colon) = _____________________

ʽ (looks like an English apostrophe) = _________________________________

There are five Greek accent marks:

The first two marks are called breathing marks. If a word begins with a vowel, it will always have a breathing mark.

1. ________________ breathing mark at the beginning of a word = breath sound. *Example*: ὁ (pronounced huh).
2. ________________ breathing mark has no additional sound and you should pronounce the vowel as is. *Example*: ἐ (pronounced eh).

The following three accent marks are used to indicate emphasis when you pronounce the word. Practice writing these marks in the blanks.

3. Grave = ὸ. ____________
4. Acute = ό. ____________
5. Circumflex = ῦ . ____________

There are 4 rules of syllabification (the division of words into syllables):

1. This is more of an art than a science. It is very similar to English — don't panic.
2. There is one vowel or diphthong per syllable.
3. Two vowels that are not a diphthong get divided.
4. If you can't pronounce two connected consonants, divide them.

Let's practice!

ΚΑΤΑ ΙΩΑΝΝΗΝ 1

John 1 Greek NT: Westcott / Hort (1881)

1Ἐν ἀρχῇ ἦν ὁ λόγος, καὶ ὁ λόγος ἦν πρὸς τὸν θεόν, καὶ θεὸς ἦν ὁ λόγος. 2οὗτος ἦν ἐν ἀρχῇ πρὸς
τὸν θεόν. 3πάντα δι' αὐτοῦ ἐγένετο, καὶ χωρὶς αὐτοῦ ἐγένετο οὐδὲ ἓν ὃ γέγονεν 4ἐν αὐτῷ ζωὴ
ἦν, καὶ ἡ ζωὴ ἦν τὸ φῶς τῶν ἀνθρώπων· 5καὶ τὸ φῶς ἐν τῇ σκοτίᾳ φαίνει καὶ ἡ σκοτία αὐτὸ οὐ
κατέλαβεν.

You will want to read this over and over again. It will help you immensely. So find a restaurant with a Dancing Zorba on the sign, and sit in a booth reading this to yourself until it is smooth. If you choose to read it out loud, please be aware that you might be removed from the restaurant. Pronunciation exercise. To pronounce a word:

- First, count the number of vowels.
- Then, where there are two or more vowels in succession, identify pairs of vowels that form diphthongs.
- Next, counting each diphthong as one vowel sound, and every other vowel as a vowel sound, count the total number of vowel sounds. This is the number of syllables in the word.
- Pronounce the syllables, syllable by syllable.
- Identify the syllable that has an accent mark indicating that syllable should be stressed.
- Pronounce the whole word, stressing the accented syllable.

Break down the word in the following process:

Example: οὗτος

- Count the vowels ______________________________
- Identify diphthongs ______________________________
- Count the vowel sounds ___________________________
- Pronounce each syllable ___________________________
- Identify the accented syllable ______
- Pronounce each syllable, stressing the accented syllable

Once you are comfortable reading the passage above out loud, get an interlinear translation of the Bible. There is a free version online at http://biblehub.com/interlinear/. Now read this through in the Greek several times while noticing the English translation of the verse. This is a great way to learn vocabulary words!

Application Review:

1. Write the five Greek punctuation marks, and list their function.

   1. ____ ____
   2. ____ ____
   3. ____ ____
   4. ____ ____
   5. ____ ____

2. List the five Greek accent marks, and list their function.

   1. ____ ____
   2. ____ ____
   3. ____ ____
   4. ____ ____
   5. ____ ____

3. List the four rules of syllabification.

   1. ____
   2. ____
   3. ____
   4. ____

4. Write the meaning of the following words. (Optional vocabulary memorization)

   ἀρχῇ: ____________________

   Λόγος: ____________________

   Θεόν: ____________________

   Πάντα: ____________________

   Οὗτος: ____________________

   αὐτῷ: ____________________

   ζωὴ: ____________________

   σκοτίᾳ: ____________________

Part 1: English Grammar Review

Noun: Person, place, or ____________________. *Example*: Cat.

Adjective: A word that modifies/defines/describes a ______________. *Example*: The lazy cat.

Pronoun: A word that replaces a noun/thing. *Example*: This or that.

Personal Pronoun: A word that replaces a ___________________. I, you, he, she, it.

Definite Article: The word "the," which modifies the noun identifying which. *Example*: The cat.

Indefinite Article: The word "a" which modifies a noun. *Example*: A cat.

Verb/Predicate: A word that shows ________________. *Example*: The lazy cat slept.

Be Verb: This is a ____________________ verb: Is, am, are, was, were, be, being, been.

Adverb: A word typically ending in the letters _____ and ______ that modifies a verb or noun. An adverb helps us understand where, when, why, or how something happened. *Example*: Bob ran quickly to see the lovely girl.

Adverbial Phrase: An adverbial phrase can modify an adverb, adjective, or verb. It is usually accompanied by other words (like prepositions). *Example*: The boy ran to his mother as quickly as he could.

Infinitives: A verb that functions as a ___________ to describe the action or state of something. *Example*: My mom knows how to cook.

Preposition: Shows the relationship between two words. *Example*: The cat slept with the dog.

Object of a Preposition: A noun or pronoun that follows a preposition (over, under, through, etc.) that completes its meaning. *Example*: Bob is at the movies.

Direct Object: A noun that is directly affected by the action of the _________. *Example*: Bob hit Tim.

Indirect Object: A noun that is indirectly affected by the action of the verb. *Example*: Emily gave a ball to Jack. An indirect object can usually be identified with the preposition "________" in front of it.

Predicate Nominative: A noun that is connected to the subject with a "_______" verb. Example: Haley is my daughter.

Predicate Adjective: An adjective that is connected to the subject with a "be" verb. *Example*: Haley is beautiful.

Dependent Clause: A clause that _____________ stand alone. *Example*: I like to sing while driving. ("while driving" is the dependent clause)

Independent Clause: A clause that can stand by itself. *Example*: I like to sing.

Syntax: The study of the rules for the formation of sentences in a language.

Part 2: English vs. Greek Grammar

There are many sizeable differences between the two languages.

1. W________ order.

English word order is typically: subject, verb, object. *Example*: The boy ran to the car.

In Greek, the word order is TYPICALLY subject, object, verb.

Greek word order is most often determined by what the author is trying to emphasize.

Example:

English — James is the King of England. (James appears to be emphasized)
Greek — The England of the King is James. (this stressed England)

Understanding word order in Greek is crucial.

Example: 2 Corinthians 5:21 — For our sake he made him to be sin who knew no sin, so that in him we might become the righteousness of God.

Romans 8:1 — Therefore there is now no condemnation for those who are in Christ Jesus.

2. The English language can be ______________. Example: Billy ran to his father, and he ran for help.

3. English uses a lot of words to describe when the action of a verb is taking place. *Example*: We were going. In Greek, verbs are more precise. Only one word is needed to say the same thing. This is done by changing the ending of the verb (also known as the suffix).

4. English uses a lot of words to tell us exactly how we are to understand the _________. In Greek, nouns are more precise. Only one noun is needed. This is done by changing the ending of the noun.

5. Please note, this is a Greek language class, not a math class. So have mercy on Todd for skipping number 5 on the chalkboard. Oops.

6. Greek does not need y'all, all y'all, or you guys. The personal pronoun "you" can be both singular and plural in English. Not in Greek.

7. The ______________ article is crucial.

Example: John 1:21: And they asked him, "What then? Are you Elijah?" He said, "I am not." "Are you the prophet?" And he answered, "No."

John 1:29: The next day he saw Jesus coming toward him, and said, "Behold, the Lamb of God, who takes away the sin of the world!"

Anarthrous: A noun does not have to have a definite article for it to be definite. This is called anarthrous. However, a noun that has a definite article can never be indefinite.

- The definite article can be used as a pronoun.
- The article can be used to distinguish one person from another.
- The article can turn almost any part of speech into a noun: adverbs, adjectives, prepositional phrases, particles, infinitives, participles, and even finite verbs.

Was Jesus created in "a beginning" or in the beginning? John 1:1: In the beginning was the Word, and the Word was with God, and the Word was God.

Was John the Baptist sent from "a god" or God? John 1:6: There was a man sent from God, whose name was John.

The Granville Sharp ______________: When two non-personal nouns (the Lord and Savior) are connected by the conjunction "and," and the first noun has a definite article and the second does not, then both nouns are referring to the same person.

- Titus 2:13: "Awaiting our blessed hope, the appearing of the glory of our great God and Savior Jesus Christ."
- 2 Peter 1:1: "To those who have obtained a faith of equal standing with ours by the righteousness of our God and Savior Jesus Christ."

Application Review:

1. What do you think Todd means by the "fullness of time concept"?

2. English word order is typically: ___________, ___________, ___________

3. In Greek, the word order is TYPICALLY: ___________, ___________, ___________

4. Look up the following verses. What rule do they all have in common? 2 Peter 1:1, 1:11, 2:20, 3:2, and 3:18 .

5. Now look up Romans 3:21 and 15:4. How do these verses differ from the ones in question 4 above?

6. Write the meaning of the following words. (Optional vocabulary words)

Νυνὶ

δικαιοσύνη

Μαρτυρουμένη

προφητῶν

Subjective noun: S____________________

Objective noun: O____________________

Possessive noun: P____________________

CASE:

In Greek, there are five cases that tell us exactly how a noun is to be used in a sentence. In English, the word "typewriter" is always typewriter. You know how to understand "typewriter" based on how it is used in the sentence.

In Greek, the word order can change based on what the author wants to stress. So a Greek sentence might read: Old is the typewriter. Typewriter is still the subject, but it appears at the end of the sentence. How do you know typewriter is the subject? Because it will appear in the subject case.

There are __________ cases in Greek:

Nominative: The _________________________ case.

Genitive: There are many uses, but it is typically known as the ______________________ case.

Dative: Mostly it is the ________________________ object case.

Accusative: Mostly the _____________________ object case.

Vocative: The case of address (the endings never change with proper nouns).

To DECLINE a noun is to take the stem of the noun and then change the _______________ to match the case, or in other words, when you say the noun and give all of the endings for each case.

With Greek nouns, the stem of the noun "cat" always stays the same, but the endings change to tell us something more specific about the use of the word "cat."

Note: In English, "cat" can be the subject, object or indirect object, or the object of a preposition. In Greek, the word "cat" takes on a different ending to tell us exactly what its usage is and how to understand it. This is important because the word order in Greek does not follow the English pattern of subject, verb, object. Greek word order is based on the emphasis the author is trying to make. Therefore, the word order can be wildly different, and the only way to know how each word is to be understood is through its ending.

English word: cat	Singular	Plural
Nominative	catus	catī
Genitive	catī	catōrum
Dative	catō	catīs
Accusative	catum	catos

Declensions. There are three basic inflectional patterns that a word can follow. Each of these patterns is called a "declension." Which pattern a word follows has no effect on its meaning, only its form.

- Nouns that have a stem ending in an alpha or eta are first declension, take first declension endings, and are primarily feminine.
- Nouns that have a stem ending in an omicron are second declension, take second declension endings, and are mostly masculine or neuter.
- If the stem of a word ends in a consonant, it is third declension.

NUMBER: As in English, nouns are either singular or ______________________.

GENDERS: There are three genders in Greek: masculine, ____________________, and neuter. All nouns have a specific gender, but these genders are not predictable. Things (including concrete objects and abstract ideas) can be masculine, feminine, or neuter, and there is no way to predict the gender. For example, the wall is masculine, the door is feminine, and the floor is neuter.

It is important to understand genders, as the ending of the noun and its adjective must match.

The definite article ending will also change by case. Thankfully, the ending of the definite article is typically the same as the ending of the noun.

Latin has ______________ declensions, but Greek only has three, so count your blessings.

PARSING: Stating the nouns. Case, number, gender, lexical meaning (dictionary form).

A ________________ is a Greek dictionary.

When you memorize a Greek noun, you will memorize the nominative singular, genitive singular, and the nominative definite article. This will help you to know to which declension the noun belongs so you can identify the right endings.

Application Review:

1. List the five Greek cases and their general action:
   1. ______________, ______________
   2. ______________, ______________
   3. ______________, ______________
   4. ______________, ______________
   5. ______________, ______________
2. What does it mean to decline a noun?

3. For further study, pdf worksheets, and online exercises you can visit: www.inthebeginning.org/ntgreek

Review from the last lesson.

FIVE CASES:

- **Nominative:** Subject case.
- **Genitive:** Possession or ______________________ case.
- **Dative:** ____________________ object case.
- **Accusative:** Direct ____________________ case.
- **Vocative:** Proper name, address, or exclamation.

There are three different declensions with three different endings for each case.

Parsing identifies the case, number, and gender of a ______________________.

Declining is putting the correct ending on a ____________________ in each case.

Now, let's look at the different cases in more detail.

VOCATIVE: Case of address, proper name, or for expressing an exclamation. Sometimes this is a simple address, "Our Father, who art in heaven," or an emotional address, "Jerusalem, Jerusalem!"

The vocative is the least commonly used case.

NOMINATIVE: The nominative is mostly used as the subject, which "names" the main subject of the sentence.

- **Predicate Nominative:** When a linking verb (is, am, are, etc.) connects the subject with another noun. *Example*: John 4:24 — God is spirit.
- **Nominative in Apposition:** When two subject-like words are linked together. *Example*: Christ the Lord or John the Baptist.
- **Parenthetic Nominative:** Typically a parenthetic clause that describes another ___________ or noun. *Example*: John 1:6 — There came a man sent from God (his name was John).

GENITIVE: The Possession or Descriptive Case. The "of" case (but 14 other prepositions can be used: from, around, away, under, beside, upon, over, in, into, down, through, towards, with, before).

The Genitive Case DESCRIBES something! Genitive is possibly the most important case in Greek as it clarifies and qualifies so many things.

The word "of" is usually involved in the translation of a genitive.

There are _______ different uses of the genitive case. Here are the major uses.

- **Genitive of Subordination:** Shows the relationship of one entity over another. *Example*: Matthew 9:34 — The ruler over demons.

  Colossians 1:15b. Christ is πρωτότοκος πάσης κτίσεως, "the firstborn of all creation." Jehovah's Witnesses and some others press this to mean that Christ was a created thing, simply the first created thing. If true, then He is not God. However, "firstborn" is a title, not when you were born. The genitive does not indicate that of which He is a member, but the category over which He is Firstborn. Only thus does the next clause ("For by him all things were created, etc.") make any sense — that is, it makes no sense to say, "He was the first created thing, because everything was created by Him." The genitive of subordination specifies that which is subordinated to or under the dominion of the head noun. Therefore, firstborn is not a part of the creation, but the firstborn (pre-eminent one) is the head of the creation. Hence, Jesus is not a part of the creation, because the creation is subordinated to Him.

- **Genitive of Possession:** Possessive Genitive — Showing ____________ or possession. To determine if it is the Genitive of Possession, try substituting the word "of" with "belonging to" or "possessed by." *Example*: John 1:29 — "Behold the Lamb of God." Or Hebrews 11:25 — "the people of (belonging to) God."

- **Subjective Genitive:** Describes the verb, acts as the subject of the verb. *Example*: Coming of the Son of Man.

- **Objective Genitive:** Describes the verb, acts as the direct object of the verb. This genitive is the object of an action or feeling expressed by a noun or adjective. *Example*: Blasphemy of the Holy Spirit.

- **Descriptive Genitive (Attributive Genitive):** Describes the noun. Describes an attribute or quality to the noun, like an adjective but with stronger emphasis. It is very common in the New Testament. *Example*: Day of salvation or the body of sin.

- **Partitive Genitive:** Shows the whole of which the subject is a part. Partitive Genitive indicates the whole of the noun. Substitute "of" with "which is a part of." The partitive indicates a part of a whole: a piece of cake or a portion of you. *Example*: Luke 19:8 — "half of my possessions."
- **Appositional or Epexegetical Genitive:** Denotes equality. The cities of Sodom and Gomorrah. *Example*: Matthew 2:11 — "They saw the child with Mary, his mother."

  Simple Apposition

  Example: Colossians 1:18 — "He is the head of the body, (namely) the church."

  Epexegetical Genitive — This use of the genitive helps to define a vague noun.

  Example: 2 Corinthians 5:5 — "Who has given to us the down payment of the Spirit."
- **Genitive of Origin:** Describes the source. *Example*: Obedience that comes from faith.
- **Genitive of Contents or Genitive of Material:** Describes what the subject is made of, or the contents of an object. *Example*: A net full of fish; a cup of water.
- **Genitive of Measure:** Denotes measure of space, time, or value. *Example*: A journey seven miles long.
- **Genitive of Relationship:** Indicates a familial relationship. *Example*: The mother of Jesus.
- **Genitive of Agent:** Indicates the agent or doer of an action. *Example*: Miracles were done by Him.
- **Genitive of Source:** Indicates where something comes from or the source of something. *Example*: Romans 15:4 — "the comfort of (derived from) the scriptures."
- **Genitive of Time:** Describes when something happened. *Example*: John 3:2 — "he came to Jesus during the night"
- **Genitive of Comparison:** Used to compare objects. *Example*: Matthew 6:25 — "Is not your life worth more than food?"
- **Attributive Genitive:** Describes an attribute or quality. *Example*: Romans 6:6 — This body of sin.
- **Genitive of Association:** Describes the one with whom the subject is related. *Example*: Romans 8:17 — "heirs with Christ."
- **Genitive of Comparison:** Like more, less, or greater. *Example*: Matthew 3:1 — "He is mightier than I." Matthew 6:25 — "Is not your life (worth) more than food?" Usually comes after a comparative adjective (less, greater). Usually "of" is replaced with "than."
- **Plenary Genitive:** Indicating both Subjective and Objective Genitives at the same time. The author can use ambiguity to convey a deeper meaning. *Example*: 2 Corinthians 5:14 — "the love of Christ constrains us." Christ's love for us and our love for Him is constraining us.

Bottom Line: Genitive DESCRIBES something!!!!!!!!

Application Review:

1. The nominative case is mostly used as the __________.
2. The vocative is the case of __________________, ____________ __________, or expressing an ____________________.
3. The genitive is also known as the "____" case, but other ______________ can also be used.

   The Greek language helps us understand so much about what the author is trying to communicate by the use of nouns in their cases. The three declensions, or endings within each case help us understand how the noun is to be used i.e., whether it is singular or plural and its gender.

Dative: The in________________ object case or the p______________________ case.

Second only to the genitive case in the number of uses, the dative case is typically known as the indirect object case (the "to" case). There are over a dozen other uses of the dative case.

The Indirect Object or Personal Case or the "to" case. The dative typically indicates the person for whom something is done.

Indirect Object: When the verb is in the active voice, the indirect object receives the direct object ("the batter hit the ball to me"); when the verb is in the passive voice, the indirect object receives the subject of the verb ("the ball was hit to me").

Example: John 4:10 — "and he would have given to you living water"

Dative of Means/Instrument: The means (or the instrument) by which something is done. The prepositions with, by, or by means of can be used to translate this use of the dative.

Example: John 11:2 — "She wiped His feet with [by means, by the instrument of] her hair."

Example: Ephesians 2:8–9 — "By grace [by the means of] are you saved through faith."

Matthew 8:16 — "and He cast out the spirits with a word." He didn't need dances, prances, incense, or instruments, nor was it usually an involved process. He only had one instrument: His word. A word from Jesus and bam! They're gone.

Indirect Object: Your key word is "to." *Example*: He threw the ball to Jack.

Dative of Place Where or Locative Dative: This use shows the location of an item or in which an action takes place. Although it can be translated by the prepositions in, on, at, upon, or beside, the locative dative is best translated by the phrase "in the sphere of" or "in the realm of."

Example: Matthew 5:3 "Blessed are the poor in (the realm of) spirit."

Dative of Time: Describes when an event takes place. *Example*: Matthew 20:19 — "on the third day He will be raised."

Dative of Advantage: Indicates the meaning "for the benefit of" or "in the interest of."

Example: 2 Corinthians 5:13 — "For if we are beside ourselves, it is for God; if we are in our right minds, it is for you."

Dative of Disadvantage: Can be translated "to the detriment of" or "against." *Example*: Matthew 23:31 — "you testify against yourselves."

Dative of Association: Indicates the person or thing one associates with or accompanies. It can be translated in English with the phrase "in association with." *Example*: Ephesians 2:5 — "he made us alive together (in association) with Christ."

Dative of Interest: Indicates the person interested in the verbal action. *Example*: Revelation 21:2 — "prepared as a bride adorned for her husband."

Dative of Degree of Difference: Denotes the degree of difference between two things being compared. *Example*: She is younger than you.

Dative of Reference . . . with reference: *Example*: Romans 6:11 — "Consider yourselves to be dead to sin, but alive to God."

Dative of Sphere: Indicates the sphere or realm in which the word to which it is related takes place or exists. *Example*: Acts 16:5 — "The churches grew in faith."

Dative of Manner (Adverbial Dative): Denotes the manner in which the action of the verb is accomplished. Answers the question, "How?" *Example*: John 7:26 — "He speaks with boldness."

Dative of Cause: Indicates the cause or basis of the action of the verb. *Example*: Luke 15:17 — "How many of my father's hirelings are overflowing in bread, but I am perishing here because of a famine?"

Accusative: The direct object case, the accusative does have some additional uses (but mercifully, not as many as the genitive and dative).

When you think accusative, think "limits the action of a verb." It has a DIRECT link to the verb, which helps me understand the verb better.

Direct Object: Indicates the immediate object of the action of a transitive verb. It receives the action of the verb. It limits the verbal action. *Example*: He threw the ball to David. ("Threw" is the verb and "ball" is the direct object of the verb and the accusative case.)

Predicate Accusative: A transitive verb (not a "be" verb) that connects the subject and the (direct) object. *Example*: Matthew 22:3 — "He sent his servants to call those who had been invited." Hebrews 5:12 — "You need someone to teach you."

Adverbial Accusative (Accusative of Manner): Acts like an adverb because it qualifies the action of the verb rather than the quantity or extent of the action. *Example*: Matthew 6:33 — "but seek first the kingdom of God."

Accusative of Measure (Extent of Time or Space): Indicates the extent of the verbal action. This can either be how far (extent of space) or for how long (extent of time). *Example*: Matthew 20:6 — "Why have you been standing here idle the whole day?"

Accusative of Respect: Indicates with reference to what extent the verbal action is represented as true. *Example*: John 6:10 — "So the men sat down, [with reference to] number about five thousand."

Accusative of Place to Which: With certain prepositions indicates where the subject is headed. *Example*: He went into the wilderness to pray.

Application Review:

1. The dative case is the __________________ ____________________ case, or it is telling me about the ______________________ who is doing something.
2. The dative case is also known as the "______" case.
3. The accusative is the _____________ _____________ case.
4. The accusative case limits the action of a __________.

Part 1. Verb parts

Verbs are like nouns, only completely different. Verbs are ______________ words.

In Greek, the verb tells us not only when the action happens, it also tells how it happened and the effect of the action! Greek focuses more on the ____________ than the when.

In Greek, we DECLINE nouns, but we __________________ verbs.

To conjugate is to change the ending (suffix) and sometimes the beginning (the prefix) and that tells us how the verb is to be understood . . . all in one little word!

There are __________ basic parts (or aspects) that are indicated by every Greek verb form. They are: person, number, tense, voice, and mood.

1. **Number:** There are ___________ numbers in Greek verbs, singular and plural. These will always agree with the subject.
2. **Person:** Indicates the individual who is performing the action.

   First person singular: _____

   Second person singular: _______

   Third person singular: _____, _____, ____

   First person plural: _____

   Second person plural: _____

   Third person plural: _____
3. **Tense:** When the action takes place: past, present, future. It will also tell us HOW the action takes place: continuous, one time, one time with ongoing effects.
4. **Voice**: Describes the relationship between the verb and the subject. The voice determines if the subject is doing the action or receiving the action.

   Active: The subject is performing the action. *Example*: Jesus healed the blind man.

   Middle Voice: The subject is acting upon himself. *Example*: I am dressing myself.

   Passive: The subject is acted upon. *Example*: The blind man was healed by Jesus.
5. **Mood**: While tense deals with the kind of action of a verb, MOOD tells us about the certainty (or lack thereof) of the action. There are four moods:

   Indicative: The action actually happens.

   Imperative: A c___________________. This is the least certain of the four moods. You hope something is going to happen.

   Subjunctive: The p___________________ mood, it might happen. Let us go on vacation.

   Optative: The "hope" mood.

Part 2. More about tenses

Tense: There are three kinds of action in Greek:

1. Continuous action.
2. Completed action with ongoing results.
3. Simple occurrence with no ongoing results.

Tense: There are s____________________ tenses.

Kind of Action and Time of Action for Each Verb Tense

Tense Name	Kind of Action (how)	Time Element (in Indicative Mood)
Present	progressive or "continuous"	present continuous action
Aorist	simple occurrence	past completed action
Perfect	completed, with results	past, with present results
Imperfect	progressive or "continuous"	past over extended time
Future	simple occurrence	future
Past Perfect	completed, with results	past complete
Future Perfect	completed, with results	future with results

Present Tense: Shows ________________ action with no future end in sight: I am going. The present tense actually has a range of present activities.

Present: The action is happening right now. *Example*: You are healed.

Progressive Present: Action that is in progress. Sometimes the present can indicate activity that is happening over a period of time. *Example*: Luke 15:29 — "I have served you for these many years."

Repeated Present: An action that happens repeatedly. *Example*: Matthew 7:7 — "Ask . . . seek . . . knock."

Historical Present: When the author is trying to place the reader in an event that has already taken place. *Example*: Matthew 26:40 — "He came to his disciples and found them sleeping, and he said. . . ."

Futuristic Present: The present tense to describe a future event. *Example*: John 4:25 — Messiah is coming.

Two Present Examples:

I John 3:8–9 — "He who commits sin is of the devil." The present tense tells us that the sinning action must be ongoing, continuous. In other words, Christians sin, but they do not live a lifestyle of perpetual, ongoing sin.

Ephesians 5:18 — "Be filled with the Spirit."

Aorist Tense has historically been the punctiliar tense, describing a ________ event in the past like the English past tense. This is the snapshot tense, a past event with no ongoing results. Recently, scholars teach that it is simply showing that something happened, but not how or the effect.

The truth is, the aorist "simply refers to the action itself without specifying whether the action is unique, repeated, ingressive, instantaneous, past, or accomplished" (Carson, *Exegetical Fallacies*, p. 70).

The difference between the aorist and the perfect may be seen by comparing Acts 2:2 and Acts 5:38. "A sound *filled* [aorist] the whole house" (Acts 2:2), but "You have filled [perfect] Jerusalem with your teaching" (Acts 5:38).

Example of the aorist: "He who has begun a good work in you will complete it until the day of Christ Jesus" (Phil. 1:6; NKJV).

Imperfect Tense shows continuous action that happened in the past over an ____________ period of time. While the aorist is the snapshot tense, the imperfect is the motion picture tense. Galatians 1:13 — Paul refers to his persecution of the church and describes how "I . . . tried to destroy it."

Perfect Tense is the completed past tense with ongoing effects into the present. *Example*: 1 John 5:1 — "Everyone who *believes* [present tense] that Jesus is the Christ has been born [perfect tense] of God" (ESV).

Future Tense describes an event that will happen at some time in the future. The future is the tense of expectation. *Example*: "We know that if he is manifested, we will be like Him, for we will see Him even as He is" (1 John 3:2).

Pluperfect or Past Perfect Tense is a completed event or action that happened in the past. *Example*: "and they beat against that house; and it did not fall, for it was founded on the rock" (Matt. 7:25).

The perfect and pluperfect are the same regarding the type of action; they only differ as to when the action took place. The pluperfect tells us when the activity happened, but does not help us understand the results (if any) of the action.

Future Perfect Tense describes an event that will exist in a completed state in the future. *Example*: "We will be like Him for we will see Him as He is" (1 John 3:2).

Application Review:

1. List the five basic parts that are indicated by every Greek verb form.

____

____

____

____

____

2. List the three voices in Greek.

____

____

____

3. List the four moods in Greek.

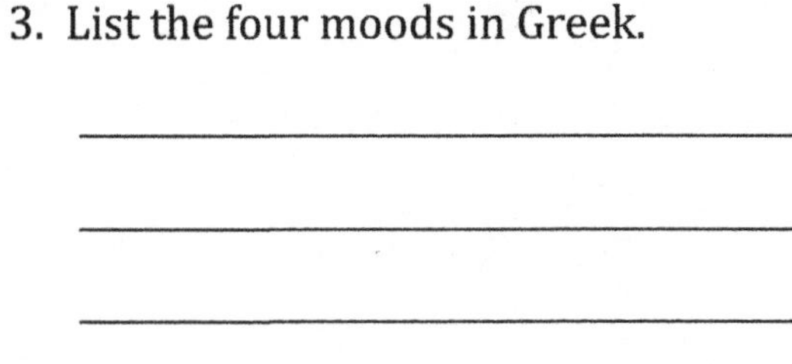

____

____

____

____

4. List the seven Greek tenses.

____

____

____

____

____

____

____

5. For additional study and an online tool for conjugating Greek verbs visit:

http://www.ibiblio.org/koine/greek/lessons/verbs%20pai.html

Review:

Person: Person identifies if the __________ is singular or plural.

The singular persons are: First (I), Second (you singular), Third (he, she, it).

The plural persons are: First (we), Second (you plural), Third (they).

Number: Singular or ____________________.

Tense: There are ________________ tenses:

1. Present: Ongoing activity in the present.
2. Aorist: A past event without specific time or results.
3. Perfect: A one-time event in the past with ongoing effects.
4. Imperfect: An ongoing past event.
5. Future: Something that will happen in the future.
6. Plu-perfect: Past event without ongoing effect.
7. Future perfect: A future event that will definitely happen.

Voice:

The voice describes who is doing or receiving the action.

Active: The ___________ is performing the action. The active voice emphasizes the action of the verb. Example: Jesus wept.

Middle: The subject is acting upon himself. While the active voice emphasizes the action of the verb, the middle voice emphasizes the subject or the one doing the action. Example: Pilate washed his hands.

Passive: The subject is acted upon.

Acts 1:5: ". . . you shall be baptized with the Holy Spirit."

Ephesians 5:18 — "Be (being) filled with the Holy Spirit." The present tense tells us that being filled with the Spirit is not a one-time event. Furthermore, it is an imperative (command), passive (we don't do it, it is done to us), present (continuous): a better translation would be: Be being filled with the Spirit.

1 Corinthians 1:18 — "The word of the cross is folly to those who are perishing, but to us who are being saved it is the power of God."

2 Corinthians 2:15 — "For we are the aroma of Christ to God among those who are being saved and among those who are perishing."

While the active voice emphasizes the action of the verb, the middle voice emphasizes the ________________ or the one doing the action.

More examples of the Passive Voice (not on the DVD):

Luke 11:38 — "When the Pharisee saw this, he was amazed because [Jesus] did not first **have himself washed** before the meal."

Acts 22:16 — "Rise, **have yourself baptized** and allow your sins **to be washed away.**"

Moods:

Mood determines whether the event is actual or merely possible. Is the idea/action a fact, or is it only possible? Mood is the way an author portrays the relation of the action to reality.

The Indicative Mood: The indicative mood states a fact. This is the mood of ____________________. There are many different types of indicative moods. **Interrogative Indicative:** The mood asks a question that expects a response of fact.

Matthew 27:11 — "Are you the King of the Jews?"

Conditional Indicative: If/Then statements.

John 5:46 — "If you believed Moses. . . ."

Declarative Indicative: The most common use of the indicative simply states a fact.

John 1:1 — "In the beginning was the Word."

There are several other lesser-used indicatives. Don't memorize these, just understand the concept. Why is this important? Because in Greek grammar, a change of mood can change the meaning of the sentence.

The Imperative Mood: The imperative mood is the mood of __________________. It is the mood furthest removed from certainty.

Imperatives can be a Command:

Mark 2:14 — "Follow me!"

Prohibition: To forbid in the form of a negative command:

Matthew 6:3 — "Do not let your left hand know what your right hand is doing."

Request or polite command, typically addressed to a superior or God.

Matthew 6:10-11 — "Let your kingdom come, let your will be done . . . give us today our daily bread."

The Subjunctive Mood: The mood of ________________________. This mood indicates that the verb will possibly happen.

Hortatory Subjunctive: Let us do something. Let us pray.

Hina + the Subjunctive: In order that. This is a very common Greek use, and it appears in seven different forms: Purpose, result, purpose-result, substantival, complementary, and command. There are even more subjunctive uses (deliberative, emphatic negation, prohibitive), but you get the point.

The Optative Mood: The "possible/potential/wish mood."

There are less than 70 uses of the optative in the NT, but its impact is powerful.

Romans 3:3–4 — "If some did not believe, their unbelief will not nullify the faithfulness of God, will it? **May it never be!** But let God be found true, and every man be found a liar."

Parsing: When you parse, you describe everything about the verb. There are five parts.

Person: 1, 2, 3, singular or plural (I, you, he/she/it, we, you, they).

Number: singular or plural.

Voice: active (does the acting), middle (acts upon itself) or passive (is acted upon).

Tense: present, imperfect, past, future, perfect, pluperfect, future perfect.

Mood: indicative, subjunctive, optative, imperative, infinitive.

Παυομαι: 1st person, singular, present, indicative, Middle/Passive.

Επαυεσθε: 2nd person, plural, imperfect, indicative, Middle/Passive.

Infinitives: Infinitives are verb forms translated with the word ______. It is like a verbal noun. It is always singular. There are (*surprise*) many forms of infinitives.

Purpose: To describe the goal of the action. It answers the question, "Why?" It is typically translated: *to, in order to, for the purpose of.*

Result: To describe the result of an action, the emphasis is put on the effort and is typically translated *so that, so as to, with the result that.*

Luke 19:10 — "I came to seek and to save that which is lost."
Matthew 5:17 — "Do not think I came **to destroy** the law."

Luke 5:7 — "They . . . filled both the boats **so that they began to sink.**"
Philippians 1:21 — "For to me, to live is Christ, and **to die** is gain."

Participle:

The participle is a declinable verbal adjective, usually ending with an __________.

John 4:11 — "that **living** water"

Hebrews 10:37 — "The **coming** One will come and will not delay."

1 Timothy 6:15 — "the king of those **who are reigning** and lord of those **who are lording it over** others."

εἰμι: **be verbs** — is, am, are, was, were, be, being, been — appearing 2,460 times in various forms in the Greek New Testament.

John 1:1

ἐν	ἀρχῇ	ἦν	ὁ	λόγος,
en	archē	ēn	o	logos
in	beginning	was	the	word

Acts 2:38 – "Then Peter said unto them, Repent, and be baptized every one of you in the name of Jesus Christ for the remission of sins, and ye shall receive the gift of the Holy Ghost."

Μετανοισατε, 2 per., pl., aor., impera. of Μετανοια , repent.

Βαπτισθετο, 3 per., sg., aor., imperat., pass., Βαπτιςο, to baptize.

A passive act never secures a direct result, but is always the result of a previous active act. Repent is a plural verb, active voice, second person, has you for its subject, and was addressed to the whole crowd. Be baptized is a singular verb, passive voice, third person, and has for its subject, not the whole crowd, but only such as had repented and believed. For **remission** does not modify both verbs. It modifies **baptized** only, and means that everyone who has repented and trusted in Christ is commanded to be baptized because his sins are remitted.

In Acts 2:38, the main verb is μετανοισατε (change mind), the aorist direct imperative (a command) of μετανοια which means to repent (change mind). This refers to that initial repentance of the sinner unto salvation. The verb translated "be baptized" is in the indirect passive imperative (a command to receive; hence, passive voice in Greek) of Βαπτιςο, which does not give it the same direct command implied in "repent."

For

The preposition "for" in the phrase "for the remission of sins" in Greek is "ειζ," unto or into, and it is in the accusative case (direct object). It can mean "for the purpose of identifying you with the remission of sins." It is the same preposition we find in 1 Corinthians 10:2 in the phrase "and were baptized unto Moses."

Ephesians 2:8–9 – "For by grace you have been saved through faith. And this is not your own doing; it is the gift of God, not a result of works, so that no one may boast."

Σεσσμενοι is a verb.

Perfect Tense: Completed in the past, results in the present

Participle Mood: Indicating a full completion, a reality

Passive Voice: The subject receives the action — the subject is NOT the performer of the action

Second Person: Applies to the person reading it

Plural Number: All may receive, "we," no exceptions

Application Review:

Read Philippians 2:5–11 again, using commentaries and Greek lexicons to help better clarify the text. You might discover some insights similar to the following concerning certain Greek words:

In verse 6, the Greek word translated "form" (*morphe*) suggests the outward manifestation that relates to the essence of something. *Morphe* occurs only twice in the New Testament and both times in this hymn to Christ, and can best be understood as the essential nature and character of God.

Paul also uses the Greek word *harpagmos* ("grasped"). This is the only time it's used in the New Testament. It is a noun derived from a verb that means to "snatch" or "seize." Christ was equal with God but refused to take any advantage from it in becoming a man, whereas Adam snatched at a false equality with God.

In verse 7, Paul spoke of Christ emptying Himself. The Greek word used here is *kenoo* ("emptied"), and can also mean to "pour out." Jesus voluntarily chose to pour Himself out for others by taking the "form of a bond servant."

The verse speaks of Christ, who existed in the essence of God, taking on the form of a servant. The Greek word for "taking" (*labon*) does not imply an exchange, but rather an addition. He did not lay aside His divinity, but rather placed a cloak of servanthood over His divinity.

In verse 11, the Greek word for "confess" (*exomologeo*) is used by Paul to refer to a future action. The verb is actually made up of three words: "ex," out of; "homou," together; and "logeo," to reason or speak intelligently. Here the word refers to a profession of the clear truth of the divine status of Christ.

This confession that "Jesus Christ is Lord" is at the heart of the Christian faith. This Jesus who humbled Himself is now exalted to the highest place . . . to the glory of God the Father.

Sources

Carson, D.A. *Exegetical Fallacies*. Baker Academic, 1996.

Marshall, Alfred. *The Interlinear NASB-NIV Parallel New Testament in Greek and English*. Grand Rapids, MI: Zondervan, 1963.

McReynolds, Paul R. *Word Study Greek-English New Testament: with Complete Concordance*. Wheaton, IL: Tyndale House Publishers, 1999.

Strong, James, John R. Kohlenberger III, and James A. Swanson. *The Strongest Strong's Exhaustive Concordance of the Bible*. Grand Rapids, MI: Zondervan, 2001.

Thayer, Joseph H. *Thayer's Greek-English Lexicon of the New Testament: Coded with Strong's Concordance Numbers*. Peabody, MA: Hendrickson Publishers, 1995.

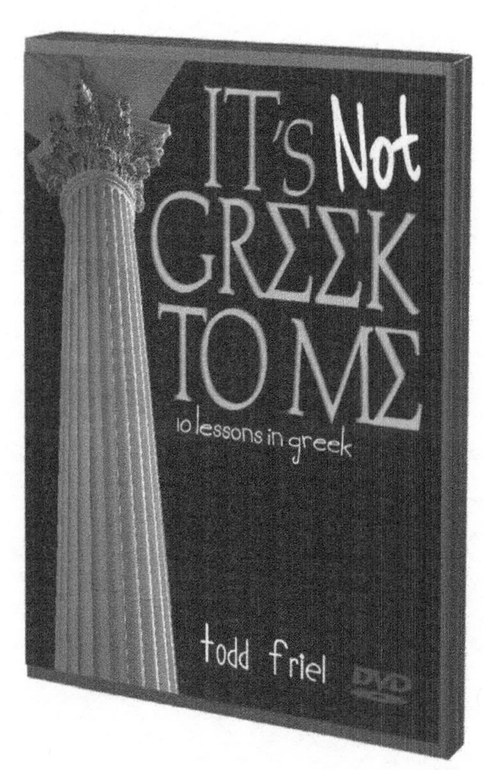

Greek Practice Sheets

for Use with

It's Not Greek To Me

DVD Learning Program

Fill in the missing Greek upper and lower case letters in the chart below.

Case		English Name	Transliteration
Upper	Lower		
		alpha	a
		beta	b
		gamma	g[1]
		delta	d
		epsilon	e
		zeta	z
		eta	ê or e
		theta	th
		iota	i
		kappa	k
		lambda	l
		mu	m
Ν	ν	nu	n
Ξ	ξ	xi	x
Ο	ο	omicron	o
Π	π	pi	p
Ρ	ρ	rho	r
Σ	ς or σ	sigma	s
Τ	τ	tau	t
Υ	υ	upsilon	u or y
Φ	φ	phi	ph
Χ	χ	chi	ch
Ψ	ψ	psi	ps
Ω	ω	omega	ô or o

Fill in the missing Greek upper and lower case letters in the chart below.

Case		English Name	Transliteration
Upper	Lower		
Α	α	alpha	a
Β	β	beta	b
Γ	γ	gamma	g[1]
Δ	δ	delta	d
Ε	ε	epsilon	e
Ζ	ζ	zeta	z
Η	η	eta	ê or e
Θ	θ	theta	th
Ι	ι	iota	i
Κ	κ	kappa	k
Λ	λ	lambda	l
Μ	μ	mu	m
		nu	n
		xi	x
		omicron	o
		pi	p
		rho	r
		sigma	s
		tau	t
		upsilon	u or y
		phi	ph
		chi	ch
		psi	ps
		omega	ô or o

Fill in the missing Greek transliteration in the chart below.

Case		English Name	Transliteration
Upper	Lower		
Α	α	alpha	
Β	β	beta	
Γ	γ	gamma	
Δ	δ	delta	
Ε	ε	epsilon	
Ζ	ζ	zeta	
Η	η	eta	
Θ	θ	theta	
Ι	ι	iota	
Κ	κ	kappa	
Λ	λ	lambda	
Μ	μ	mu	
Ν	ν	nu	
Ξ	ξ	xi	
Ο	ο	omicron	
Π	π	pi	
Ρ	ρ	rho	
Σ	ς or σ	sigma	
Τ	τ	tau	
Υ	υ	upsilon	
Φ	φ	phi	
Χ	χ	chi	
Ψ	ψ	psi	
Ω	ω	omega	

Fill in the missing English names for the Greek letters in the chart below.

Case		English Name	Transliteration
Upper	Lower		
Α	α		a
Β	β		b
Γ	γ		g[1]
Δ	δ		d
Ε	ε		e
Ζ	ζ		z
Η	η		ê or e
Θ	θ		th
Ι	ι		i
Κ	κ		k
Λ	λ		l
Μ	μ		m
Ν	ν		n
Ξ	ξ		x
Ο	ο		o
Π	π		p
Ρ	ρ		r
Σ	ς or σ		s
Τ	τ		t
Υ	υ		u or y
Φ	φ		ph
Χ	χ		ch
Ψ	ψ		ps
Ω	ω		ô or o

Fill in the missing Greek vowels in the chart below.

Greek Vowels	
Short	Long
– as in father	– same only held longer
– as in sled	– as in play
– as in Ontario	– as in boat
– as in fish	– as in police
– as in flute	– same only held longer

Open or Closed Greek Vowels	
Open	Closed
1.	1.
2.	2.
3.	
4.	
5.	

Fill in the Greek Dipthong in the left column. Give an example in the right column.

is pronounced ai	example: aisle
is pronounced ei	
is pronounced oi	
is pronounced ow	
is pronounced eu	
is pronounced the same as ευ	
is pronounced ou	
is pronounced uee	

Draw the five Greek punctuation marks in the boxes below and then write the name of the similar punctuation in the English language:

____________ ____________ ____________ ____________ ____________

What are the two types of breathing marks?

1. ________________________

2. ________________________

Name the following examples of the five Greek accent marks.

1. ὁ ________________________

2. ό ______________________________

3. ῦ _______________________________

4. ἐ _______________________________

5. ὸ _______________________________

Write the four rules of syllabification:

1.

2.

3.

4.

Choose from the following words and phrases to match the definitions below.

Definite article
Noun
Pronoun
Personal pronoun
Verb/predicate
Be verb
Adverbial phrase
Preposition
Object of a preposition
Direct object
Adjective
Indirect object
Predicate adjective
Dependent clause
Independent clause
Syntax
Indefinite article
Predicate nominative
Adverb
Infinitive

______________________ - The word "the", which modifies the noun identifying which.

______________________ - The word "a" which modifies a noun

______________________ - A word that shows action

______________________ - This is a connecting verb

______________________ - A word typically ending in the letters "l" and "y" that modifies a verb or noun and helps us understand where, when, why, or how something happened

______________________ - A phrase that modifies an adverb, adjective, or verb. It is usually accompanied by other words (like prepositions)

______________________ - A verb that functions as a noun to describe the action or state of something

______________________ - Shows the relationship between two words

______________________ - A noun or pronoun that follows a preposition (over, under, through, etc.) that completes its meaning

______________________ - A noun that is directly affected by the action of the verb

______________________ - A noun that is indirectly affected by the action of the verb. *Example*: Emily gave a ball to Jack. This type of noun can usually be identified with the preposition "to" in front of it.

______________________ - A noun that is connected to the subject with a "be" verb

______________________ - An adjective that is connected to the subject with a "be" verb

______________________ - A clause that cannot stand alone

______________________ - A clause that can stand by itself

______________________ - The study of the rules for the formation of sentences in a language

Word Order:

1. What is the typical word order for Greek? ________
   a. Subject, object, verb
   b. Verb, subject, object
   c. Object, verb, subject
   d. Subject, verb, object

2. What is the typical word order for English? ________
   a. Subject, object, verb
   b. Verb, subject, object
   c. Object, verb, subject
   d. Subject, verb, object

Circle the correct answer.

3. In which of these two languages are verbs more precise?
   English   Greek

4. Personal pronouns are always singular and plural for both Greek and English.
   True   False

5. What the author is trying to emphasize most often determines the word order in Greek.
   True   False

6. Anarthrous means a noun has to have a definite article for it to be definite.
   True   False

Fill in the English word or phrase in the left column.

	Θεόν
	Πάντα
	Οὗτος
	αὐτῷ
	ζωὴ
	σκοτίᾳ
	Νυνὶ
	Δικαιοσύνη
	Μαρτυρουμένη
	προφητῶν

Fill in the missing Greek words in the blank spaces in the following partial verse:

In	beginning	was	the	word	and	the	word	was	with	the	God
		ἦν	ὁ		καὶ	ὁ		ἦν		τὸν	

Find three examples from Scripture for the following; the object is to be familiar with the concept, and this practice sheet is an opportunity to find other examples. If time is a contraint, limit yourself to finding at least one example of each:

Vocative:

1. ____________________

2. ____________________

3. ____________________

Nominative:

1. ____________________

2. ____________________

3. ____________________

Predicate Nominative:

1. ____

2. ____

3. ____

Nominative in Apposition:

1. ____

2. ____

3. ____

Parenthetic Nominative:

1. ____

2. ____

3. ____

Find three examples from Scripture for the following; the object is to be familiar with the concept, and this practice sheet is an opportunity to find other examples. If time is a contraint, limit yourself to finding at least one example of each:

Genitive:

1. ______________________________

2. ______________________________

3. ______________________________

Genitive of Subordination:

1. ______________________________

2. ______________________________

3. ______________________________

Genitive of Possession:

1. ______________________________

2. ______________________________

3. ______________________________

Subjective Genitive:

1. ______________________________

2. ______________________________

3. ______________________________

Objective Genitive:

1. ______________________________

2. ______________________________

3. ______________________________

Descriptive Genitive (Attributive Genetive):

1. ______________________________

2. ______________________________

3. ______________________________

Find three examples from Scripture for the following; the object is to be familiar with the concept, and this practice sheet is an opportunity to find other examples. If time is a contraint, limit yourself to finding at least one example of each:

Dative:

1. ______________________________

2. ______________________________

3. ______________________________

Indirect Dative:

1. ______________________________

2. ______________________________

3. ______________________________

Dative of Means/Instrument:

1. ______________________________

2. ______________________________

3. ______________________________

Indirect Object:

1. ______________________________

2. ______________________________

3. ______________________________

Dative of Place Where or Locative Dative:

1. ______________________________

2. ______________________________

3. ______________________________

Find three examples from Scripture for the following; the object is to be familiar with the concept, and this practice sheet is an opportunity to find other examples. If time is a contraint, limit yourself to finding at least one example of each:

Dative of Time:

1. ______________________________

2. ______________________________

3. ______________________________

Dative of Advantage:

1. ______________________________

2. ______________________________

3. ______________________________

Dative of Disadvantage:

1. ______________________________

2. ______________________________

3. ______________________________

Dative of Association:

1. ______________________________

2. ______________________________

3. ______________________________

Dative of Interest:

1. ______________________________

2. ______________________________

3. ______________________________

Dative of Degree of Difference:

1. ______________________________

2. ______________________________

3. ______________________________

Find three examples from Scripture for the following; the object is to be familiar with the concept, and this practice sheet is an opportunity to find other examples. If time is a contraint, limit youself to finding at least one example of each:

Dative of Reference:

1. ____________________

2. ____________________

3. ____________________

Dative of Sphere:

1. ____________________

2. ____________________

3. ____________________

Dative of Manner (Adverbial Dative):

1. ____________________

2. ____________________

3. ____________________

Dative of Clause:

1. ____________________

2. ____________________

3. ____________________

Accusative:

1. ______________________________

2. ______________________________

3. ______________________________

Adverbial Accusative (Accusative of Manner):

1. ______________________________

2. ______________________________

3. ______________________________

Accusative of Measure (Extent of Time or Space):

1. ______________________________

2. ______________________________

3. ______________________________

Accusative of Respect:

1. ______________________________

2. ______________________________

3. ______________________________

Accusative of Place to Which:

1. ______________________________

2. ______________________________

3. ______________________________

List the three kinds of action found in Greek verbs.

1. ______________________________

2. ______________________________

3. ______________________________

Fill in the missing information in the chart below. Do the exercise after you have memorized the chart on page 53 of the Teacher Guide.

Tense Name	Kind of Action (How)	Time Element (In Indicative Mood)
Present		
Aorist	simple occurrence	
Perfect		past, with present results
Imperfect		past over extended time
Future	simple occurrence	
Past Perfect		
Future Perfect		

Find three examples from Scripture for the following; the object is to be familiar with the concept, and this practice sheet is an opportunity to find other examples. If time is a contraint, limit youself to finding at least one example of each:

The Indicative Mood:

1. ______________________________

2. ______________________________

3. ______________________________

Interrogative Indicative:

1. ______________________________

2. ______________________________

3. ______________________________

Conditional Indicative:

1. ______________________________

2. ______________________________

3. ______________________________

Declarative Indicative:

1. ______________________________

2. ______________________________

3. ______________________________

The Imperative Mood (can be a command):

1. ______________________________

2. ______________________________

3. ______________________________

Request or polite command, typically addressed to a superior or God:

1. ______________________________

2. ______________________________

3. ______________________________

The Subjunctive Mood:

1. ______________________________

2. ______________________________

3. ______________________________

The Optative Mood:

1. ______________________________

2. ______________________________

3. ______________________________

Infinitives:

1. ______________________________

2. ______________________________

3. ______________________________

Particle:

1. ______________________________

2. ______________________________

3. ______________________________

εἰμι: Be Verbs:

1. ______________________________

2. ______________________________

3. ______________________________

Get a lexicon from your local library or church library. If you don't have access to a lexicon, there are many available online free of charge including one at www.gutenberg.org. A Greek-English Lexicon to the New Testament is written by Thomas Sheldon Green. It can be downloaded or viewed in a web browser at http://www.gutenberg.org/files/40935/40935-h/40935-h.htm. Other lexicons can be found at Google Books as well.

1. Read the introduction to the lexicon you are using. Note three important things that you learn from it:

   a. ______________________________

   b. ______________________________

   c. ______________________________

2. Do you see instances of noun and verbs like you have learned in this course? Give an example of where these are noted in the lexicon (ex. in abbreviations, explanatory charts, etc.)

   ____

3. What is the structure of your lexicon? Is it similar to a dictionary or a text book?

4. What does "Greek-English" mean in terms of this lexicon? How would an "English-Greek" lexicon be different (Hint: go to http://www.biblestudytools.com/lexicons/greek/ to see how you can find words using this website)?

Quizzes

It's Not Greek to Me Concepts & Comprehension	Quiz 1	Scope: Lessons 1–3	Total score: ____of 100	Name

True or False: (5 Points Each Question)

1. Greek is always written in capital letters.

   True False

2. There are 24 letters in the Greek alphabet just like the English alphabet.

   True False

3. Koine Greek was the "street" language of New Testament times.

   True False

4. There are seven vowels in the Greek alphabet.

   True False

5. There are always silent letters in Greek pronunciation.

   True False

6. Vowel combinations are called dipthongs.

   True False

7. There are two open vowels and four closed vowels in New Testament Greek.

   True False

8. Instead of A to Z, the Greek alphabet is alpha to omega.

   True False

9. Greek punctuation marks resemble English punctuation.

   True False

10. There are five Greek accent marks.

True False

11. There are eight rules of syllabification.

True False

12. Circumflex is a Greek accent mark.

True False

13. Two Greek accent marks are called breathing marks.

True False

14. Grave, accute, and circumflex are the Greek accent marks that indicate emphasis when you pronounce a word.

True False

15. Dipthongs need to be identified before proper pronuciation can be done.

True False

List 5 of the 6 steps to pronouncing a Greek word (each correct answer is worth 5 points):

1. ex. First, count the number of vowels

2.

3.

4.

5.

It's Not Greek to Me	Quiz 2	Scope: Lessons 4–5	Total score: ____of 100	Name
Concepts & Comprehension				

True or False: (5 Points Each Question)

1. An adverbial phrase can modify an adverb, adjective, or verb, and it is never accompanied by other words (like prepositions).

   True False

2. Infinitives are verbs that function as a noun to describe the action or state of something.

   True False

3. A direct object is a noun that is directly affected by the action of the verb.

   True False

4. A predicate Nominative is a noun that is connected to the subject with a "be" verb.

   True False

5. A predicate adjective is a verb that is connected to the subject with a "be" verb.

   True False

6. A dependent clause is a clause that can stand alone.

   True False

7. An independent clause is a clause that can stand by itself.

   True False

8. Syntax is the study of the rules for the formation of sentences in a language.

   True False

9. English word order is typically verb, subject, object.

   True False

10. In Greek, the word order is TYPICALLY subject, object, verb.

    True False

11. Greek word order is not determined by what the author is trying to emphasize.

    True False

12. Understanding word order in Greek is crucial.

    True False

13. In Greek, verbs and nouns are more precise than in English.

    True   False

14. Anarthrous is a noun that does not have to have a definite article for it to be definite. However, a noun that has a definite article can never be indefinite.

    True   False

15. The Granville Sharp Rule is when two non-personal nouns are connected by the conjunction "and," and the first noun has a definite article and the second does not, then both nouns are referring to the same person.

    True   False

16. Nouns in Greek can be subjective, objective, and posssessive.

    True   False

17. In Greek, there are six cases that tell us exactly how a noun is to be used in a sentence.

    True   False

18. There are five cases in Greek: nomative, genitive, dative, accusative, and gender.

    True   False

19. To decline a noun is to take the stem of the noun and then change the ending to match the case, or in other words, when you say the noun and give all of the endings for each case.

    True   False

20. There are three genders in Greek: masculine, feminine, and neuter.

    True   False

It's Not Greek to Me / Concepts & Comprehension	Quiz 3	Scope: Lessons 6–7	Total score: ____of 100	Name

True or False: (4 Points Each Question)

1. A vocative is a case of address, proper name, or for expressing an exclamation, such as "Our Father, who art in heaven...."
   True False

2. The vocative is the most commonly used case.
   True False

3. A nominative is mostly used as the subject, which "names" the main subject of the sentence.
   True False

4. A predicate nominative is when a linking verb (is, am, are, etc.) connects the subject with another noun.
   True False

5. Christ the Lord or John the Baptist is an example of a nominative in apposition.
   True False

6. The Genitive Case DESCRIBES something and is possibly the most important case in Greek as it clarifies and qualifies so many things.
   True False

7. The word "of" is rarely involved in the translation of a genitive.
   True False

8. Genitive of Subordination shows the relationship of one entity over another.
   True False

9. To determine if a something is the Genitive of Possession, try substituting the word "of" with "belonging to" or "possessed by."
   True False

10. Subjective Genitive denotes equality.
    True False

11. Objective Genitive describes the verb, acts as the direct object of the verb. This genitive is the object of an action or feeling expressed by a noun or adjective.
    True False

12. Descriptive Genitive is the same as Attributive Genitive.
    True False

13. Partitive Genitive shows the whole of which the subject is a part. Partitive Genitive indicates the whole of the noun.

    True False

14. Appositional or Epexegetical Genitive denotes equality.

    True False

15. Second only to the genitive case in the number of uses, the dative case is typically known as the indirect object case (the "to" case).

    True False

16. "A journey seven miles long" is an example of a Genitive of Measure.

    True False

17. "He came from Bethlehem" is an example of a Genitive of Relationship.

    True False

18. Plenary Genitive indicates both Subjective and Objective Genitives at the same time.

    True False

19. Dative of Interest indicates the person interested in the verbal action.

    True False

20. Oddly, the Genitive of Agent does not indicate the agent or doer of an action.

    True False

21. Genitive of Reference indicates where something comes from or the source of something.

    True False

22. Genitive of Association describes the one with whom the subject is related.

    True False

23. Matthew 6:25 — "Is not your life worth more than food?" is an example of Genitive of Comparison.

    True False

24. Dative of Time describes when an event takes place.

    True False

25. Dative of Advantage indicates the meaning "for the benefit of" or "in the interest of," while Dative of Disadvantage can be translated "to the detriment of" or "against.

    True False

It's Not Greek to Me Concepts & Comprehension	Quiz 4	Scope: Lessons 8–10	Total score: ____of 100	Name

True or False: (4 Points Each Question)

1. In Greek, the verb tells us not only when the action happens, but it also tells how it happened and the effect of the action.

   True False

2. Person, number, tense, voice, and mood are four basic parts (or aspects) indicated by every Greek verb form.

   True False

3. Numbers in Greek verbs, singular and plural, will sometimes agree with the subject.

   True False

4. When the action takes place (past, present, future) it is known as the verb tense. It will also tell us how the action takes place: continuous, one time, one time with ongoing effects.

   True False

5. Voice describes the relationship between the verb and the time.

   True False

6. The voice determines if the subject is doing the action or receiving the action.

   True False

7. There are four types of voices: active, middle, passive, and neuter.

   True False

8. Mood tells us about the certainty (or lack thereof) of the action.

   True False

9. There are three moods in Greek: indicative, subjunctive, and optative.

   True False

10. There are three kinds of action in Greek, shown by the tense.

    True False

11. Continuous action is a tense showing a simple occurrence with no ongoing result.

    True False

12. Present action is action that is about to happen.

    True False

13. Progressive Present is action that is in progress but does not indicate activity that is happening over a period of time.

    True False

14. Matthew 26:40 — "He came to his disciples and found them sleeping, and he said. . . ." is an example of a historical present tense.

    True False

15. Futuristic Present is the present tense to describe a possible event.

    True False

16. Aorist is a future event without specific time or results.

    True False

17. Plu-perfect is a past event without ongoing effect.

    True False

18. Mood determines whether the event is actual or merely possible. Mood is the way an author portrays the relation of the action to reality.

    True False

19. Matthew 27:11 — "Are you the King of the Jews?" is an example of the indicative mood, and in particular, the interrogative indicative.

    True False

20. When you parse, you describe everything about the verb. There are three parts.

    True False

21. John 5:46 — "If you believed Moses. . . ." is an example of a declarative indicative.

    True False

22. In Greek grammar, a change of mood can change the meaning of the sentence.

    True False

23. An infinitive verb form is always singular.

    True False

24. Imperatives are usually used in a request or polite command to a superior or God.

    True False

25. The "possible/potential/wish mood" is the Optative Mood. There are less than 70 uses of the optative in the NT, but its impact is powerful.

    True False

Answer Keys

for

Worksheets, Practice Sheets,

and Quizzes

It's Not Greek to Me — Worksheet Answer Keys

Lesson One: Worksheet 1: Don't Memorize, Just Get It!

Welcome to "It's Not Greek to Me: Knowing Enough to Be Dangerous."

Your teacher has an inferiority complex and prefers to be called Mr. **Friel**.

This course is for you if:

1. You are a layperson who wants to **go deeper in studying the Word**.
2. You plan on studying **first-year** Greek.

Page 1 of Todd's Greek textbook: "Declensions: There are three declensions in Greek, instead of five as in Latin. To these, because of their general uniformity, the o-stems serve as a good introduction. In nouns of the o-declension an acute ' on the ultima in the nominative is changed to a circumflex in the genitive and dative of both numbers."

That will make sense when we are done.

What you will not learn:

1. How to ***translate***.

To translate means **to express one language into another language**.

To interpret means **to explain the meaning of the original language**.

2. Vocables = ***vocabulary***
3. Endings

Look up the word "declension." What does it mean? **Answer will vary.**

Lesson One: Worksheet 2: Don't Memorize, Just Get It!

What you will learn:

1. How to ***read*** Greek.
2. How to ***speak*** Greek.
3. How the language works. Nike says, "Just Do It!" We say, "Just ***Get*** It!"
4. How to utilize a ***concordance***.
5. How to use a ***lexicon***.
6. Your English will get "gooder." (Or more correctly, **better**!)
7. You will recognize Greek roots in many English words:

   >Ergon = **work**.

   >Adelphos = **brother**
8. Can check the Scriptures yourself to discern true from **false** teaching.
9. Get more out of **commentaries**.
10. Understand your **pastor** when he makes Greek language references.

11. **Answers will vary.**

Why did God choose this language? Give three examples. Why was this important?
1. **Specific** and **precise**; 2. Koine Greek made God's word much easier and more accessible to many people; 3. **Global**.

12. You will love your ***Savior*** more.

Lesson Two: Worksheet 1: The Alphabet

We get the word *alphabet* from the first two letters in Greek: **alpha beta**

Lesson Two: Worksheet 2: The Alphabet

Upper Case	Lower Case	English Name
Α	α	**alpha**
Β	β	**beta**
Γ	γ	**gamma**
Δ	δ	**delta**
Ε	ε	**epsilon**
Ζ	ζ	**zeta**
Η	η	**eta**
Θ	θ	**theta**
Ι	ι	**iota**
Κ	κ	**kappa**
Λ	λ	**lambda**
Μ	μ	**mu**
Ν	ν	**nu**
Ξ	ξ	**xi**
Ο	ο	**omicron**
Π	π	**pi**
Ρ	ρ	**rho**
Σ	ς or σ	**sigma**
Τ	τ	**tau**
Υ	υ	**upsilon**
Φ	φ	**phi**
Χ	χ	**chi**
Ψ	ψ	**psi**
Ω	ω	**omega**

Lesson Two: Worksheet 4: The Alphabet

1. Proper dipthongs:

    1. αι , 2. ει, 3. οι, 4. αυ, 5. ευ, 6. ov, 7. Nι

2. Improper dipthongs:

    1. ᾳ, 2. ῃ, 3. ῳ

3. Greek vowels:

    1. α, 2. ε, 3. η, 4. ο, 5. ω, 6. ι, 7. υ

4. Open vowels:

    α, ε, η, ο, ω

Lesson Three: Worksheet 1: Punctuation and Practice

1. , = comma
2. . = period
3. • = semicolon
4. : = question mark
5. ʻ = apostrophe if letter drops out

Rough

Soft

Grave (ὸ)

Acute (ό)

Circumflex (ῦ)

Lesson Three: Worksheet 2: Punctuation and Practice

- 3 vowels; o,ῦ,o
- 1 diphthong; οῦ
- 2 vowel sounds; οῦ , o and therefore, 2 syllables
- (οῦ)
- (u'-tos)

Lesson Three: Worksheet 3: Punctuation and Practice

1. Five punctuation marks:

    1. , = comma
    2. . = period
    3. • = semicolon
    4. : = question mark

5. ʼ = apostrophe if letter drops out

2. Five accent marks:
   1. Rough breathing mark = breath sound. *Example*: ὁ (pronounced huh)
   2. Soft breathing mark = no additional sound. *Example*: ἐ (pronounced eh)
   3. Grave (ὸ) = emphasis in pronunciation
   4. Acute (ό) = emphasis in pronunciation
   5. Circumflex (ῦ) = emphasis in pronunciation

3. Four rules of syllabification:
   1. This is more of an art than a science.
   2. There is one vowel or diphthong per syllable.
   3. Two vowels that are not a diphthong get divided.
   4. If you can't pronounce two connected consonants, divide them.

4. Optional vocabulary words:

   ἀρχῇ = beginning

   Λόγος = word

   Θεόν = God

   Πάντα = all things

   Οὗτος = he

   αὐτῷ = him

   ζωὴ = life

   σκοτίᾳ = darkness

Lesson Four: Worksheet 1: Grammar

English Grammar Review fill in the blank answers:

thing, noun, person, action, connecting, l and y, noun, verb, to, be, cannot

Lesson Four: Worksheet 2: Grammar

English vs. Greek Grammar fill in the blank answers:

Word, unclear, noun, definite, Rule

Lesson Four: Worksheet 3: Grammar

1. What do you think Todd means by the "fullness of time concept"?

   At just the right time, God fulfilled His promise to send a Messiah. What made two thousand years ago the right time? The Greek language! God's sovereign design was to use Greek when it was the language of the entire world so every nation could understand the Good News. More than that, Greek is a far more precise language than Old Testament Hebrew, allowing for a far more precise understanding of theology. God has very good timing!

2. English word order is typically: subject, verb, object
3. In Greek, the word order is TYPICALLY: subject, object, verb
4. Look up the following verses. What rule do they all have in common? *2 Peter 1:1, 1:11, 2:20, 3:2, and 3:18*

   (The Granville Sharp Rule: When two non-personal nouns [the Lord and Savior] are connected by the conjunction "and," and the first noun has a definite article and the second does not, then both nouns are referring to the same person.)
5. Now look up Romans 3:21 and 15:4. How do these verses differ from the ones in question 4 above?

   (Romans 3:21, "by the law and the prophets," and Romans 15:4, "through the grace and through the exhortation") — both of these verses demonstrate the use of the article with BOTH nouns, thus keeping the nouns distinct from one another.
6. Optional vocabulary words:

   Νυνὶ = now

   Δικαιοσύνη = righteousness

   Μαρτυρουμένη = to bear witness

   προφητῶν = prophet

Lesson Five: Worksheet 1: Greek Nouns

Fill in the blank answers:

Subject, object, possesses, five, subject, possessive, indirect, direct, ending, plural, feminine, five, lexicon

Lesson Five: Worksheet 2: Greek Nouns

1. The five Greek cases and their general action:
    1. Nominative; Subject
    2. Genitive; Possession
    3. Dative; Indirect object
    4. Accusative; Direct object
    5. Vocative; Title or address
2. Declining a noun is when you say the noun and give all of the endings for each case.

Lesson Six: Worksheet 1: Nominative, Genitive, and Vocative

Five cases fill in the blank answers:

Descriptive, indirect, object, noun, noun, subject, 20, ownership

Lesson Six: Worksheet 2: Nominative, Genitive, and Vocative

1. Subject
2. Address, proper name, exclamation

3. of, prepositions

Lesson Seven: Worksheet 1: Dative and Accusative

Fill in the blank answers:

indirect object, person

Lesson Seven: Worksheet 2: Dative and Accusative

1. indirect object, person
2. "to"
3. direct object
4. verb

Lesson Eight: Worksheet 1: Verbs

Fill in the blank answers:

Action, how, conjugate, five, two, I, you, he/she/it, we, you, they, command, possibility

Lesson Eight: Worksheet 2: Verbs

Fill in the blank answers:

seven, continuous, single, extended

Lesson Eight: Worksheet 3: Verbs

1. Five basic parts:
    1. Person
    2. Number
    3. Tense
    4. Voice
    5. Mood

2. Three voices:
    1. Active
    2. Middle voice
    3. Passive

3. Four moods:
    1. Indicative
    2. Imperative
    3. Subjunctive

    4. Optative
4. Seven tenses:
    1. Present
    2. Aorist
    3. Perfect
    4. Imperfect
    5. Future
    6. Past perfect
    7. Future perfect

Lesson Nine: Worksheet 1: Voice and Mood

Fill in the blank answers:

Verb, plural, seven, subject, subject

Lesson Nine: Worksheet 2: Voice and Mood

Fill in the blank answers:

Certainty, command, probability, to, ing

Greek Alphabet Practice Sheets 1–4:

This is the answer chart for alphabet worksheets 1–4.

Case		English Name	Transliteration
Upper	Lower		
Α	α	alpha	a
Β	β	beta	b
Γ	γ	gamma	g[1]
Δ	δ	delta	d
Ε	ε	epsilon	e
Ζ	ζ	zeta	z
Η	η	eta	ê or e
Θ	θ	theta	th
Ι	ι	iota	i
Κ	κ	kappa	k
Λ	λ	lambda	l
Μ	μ	mu	m
Ν	ν	nu	n
Ξ	ξ	xi	x
Ο	ο	omicron	o
Π	π	pi	p
Ρ	ρ	rho	r
Σ	ς or σ	sigma	s
Τ	τ	tau	t
Υ	υ	upsilon	u or y
Φ	φ	phi	ph
Χ	χ	chi	ch
Ψ	ψ	psi	ps
Ω	ω	omega	ô or o

Greek Alphabet – Extras Practice Sheet 5:

Greek Vowels	
Short	Long
α (alpha) – as in father	α (alpha) – same only held longer
ε (epsilon) – as in sled	η (eta) – as in play
ο (omicron) – as in Ontario	ω (omega) – as in boat
ι (iota) – as in fish	ι (iota) – as in police
υ (upsilon) – as in flute	υ (upsilon) – same only held longer

The open vowels are α, ε, η, ο, ω.

The closed vowels are ι, υ.

Example: οι is a dipthong, but ιο is not. (Compare the ***oi* in Illinois** with the ***io* in Ohio**. The ***oi*** in Illin**ois** makes one vowel sound, whereas the ***i*** and ***o*** in Oh**io** are clearly two distinct sounds).

Proper Greek Dipthongs	
αι is pronounced ai	as in Thailand or aisle
ει is pronounced ei	as in eight or freight
οι is pronounced oi	as in Illinois or oil
αυ is pronounced ow	as in cow or bow
ευ is pronounced eu	as in feud or fuel
ηυ is pronounced the same as ευ	as in feud or fuel
ου is pronounced ou	as in soup or food
υι is pronounced uee	as in queen

Punctuation and Accent Marks Practice Sheet 6

These can be in any order, but they must correspond properly with the English punctuation associated with it.

,	.	·	:	ʽ
comma	period	high period	colon	apostrophe

Two types of breathing marks:

1. Rough breathing mark
2. Soft breathing mark

Five Greek accent marks:

1. Rough breathing mark
2. Acute
3. Circumflex
4. Soft breathing mark
5. Grave

Syllabification Practice Sheet 7

Four rules of syllabification:

1. This is more of an art than a science.
2. There is one vowel or diphthong per syllable.
3. Two vowels that are not a diphthong get divided.
4. If you can't pronounce two connected consonants, divide them.

Grammar Practice Sheet 8:

Definite Article
Indefinite Article
Verb/predicate
"be" verb
Adverb
Adverbial phrase
Infinitives
Preposition
Object of a preposition
Direct object
Indirect object
Predicative nominative
Predicate adjective
Dependent clause
Independent clause
Syntax

Grammar Practice Sheet 9

1. subject, object, verb
2. subject, verb, object
3. Greek
4. False
5. True
6. False

Vocabulary Review Practice Sheet 10

God	Θεόν
all things	Πάντα
he	Οὗτος
him	αὐτῷ
life	ζωὴ
darkness	σκοτίᾳ
now	Νυνὶ
righteousness	Δικαιοσύνη
to bear witness	Μαρτυρουμένη
prophet	προφητῶν

ἐν	ἀρχῇ	ἦν	ὁ	λόγος	καὶ	ὁ	λόγος	ἦν	πρὸς	τὸν	θεόν
In	beginning	was	the	word	and	the	word	was	with	the	God

Greek Nouns Practice Sheet 11

Answers will vary depending on Scripture chosen.

Greek Nouns Practice Sheet 12

Answers will vary depending on Scripture chosen.

Greek Nouns Practice Sheet 13

Answers will vary depending on Scripture chosen.

Greek Nouns Practice Sheet 14

Answers will vary depending on Scripture chosen.

Greek Nouns Practice Sheet 15

Answers will vary depending on Scripture chosen.

Greek Verbs Practice Sheet 16

1. Continuous action.

2. Completed action with ongoing results.
3. Simple occurrence with no ongoing results.

Tense Name	Kind of Action (How)	Time Element (In Indicative Mood)
Present	**progressive or "continuous"**	**present continuous action**
Aorist	simple occurrence	**past completed action**
Perfect	**completed, with results**	past, with present results
Imperfect	**progressive or "continuous"**	past over extended time
Future	simple occurrence	**future**
Past Perfect	**completed, with results**	**past complete**
Future Perfect	**completed, with results**	**future with results**

Voice and Mood Practice Sheet 17

Answers will vary depending on Scripture chosen.

Using a Lexicon Sheet 18

1. Answers will vary. Should include items like the structure, history, or cultural aspects of the language; or the purpose of a lexicon and its importance; or applications for a lexicon, etc.
2. Answers will vary depending on the lexicon used. Be sure to note specifics where things you have learned like datives or genitives are noted, etc.
3. Should be similar to a dictionary rather than a written textbook. If the students wish, they can go into the actual structure based on the table of contents if included.
4. Simply, you need to know the word in Greek to look up the English meaning, etc. An "English-Greek" lexicon works the opposite. The language listed first is the one that you look up by to find a word in a second language listed.

Quiz 1: Lessons 1–3:

1. F
2. F
3. T
4. T
5. F
6. T
7. F
8. T
9. T
10. T
11. F
12. T
13. T
14. T
15. T

List 5 of the 6 steps to prouncing a Greek word (each correct answer is worth 5 points):

1. ex. First, count the number of vowels.
2. Then, where there are two or more vowels in succession, identify pairs of vowels that form diphthongs.
3. Next, counting each diphthong as one vowel sound, and every other vowel as a vowel sound, count the total number of vowel sounds. This is the number of syllables in the word.
4. Pronounce the syllables, syllable by syllable.
5. Identify the syllable that has an accent mark indicating that syllable should be stressed.
6. Pronounce the whole word, stressing the accented syllable.

Quiz 2: Lessons 4–5:

1. F
2. T
3. T
4. T
5. F
6. F
7. T
8. T
9. F
10. T
11. F
12. T
13. T
14. T
15. T
16. T
17. F
18. F
19. T
20. T

Quiz 3: Lessons 6–7:

1. T
2. F
3. T
4. T
5. T
6. T
7. F
8. T
9. T
10. F
11. T
12. T
13. T
14. T
15. T
16. T
17. F

18. T
19. T
20. F
21. F
22. T
23. T
24. T
25. T

Quiz 4: Lessons 8–10:

1. T
2. T
3. F
4. T
5. F
6. T
7. F
8. T
9. F
10. T
11. F
12. F
13. F
14. T
15. F
16. F
17. T
18. T
19. T
20. F
21. F
22. T
23. T
24. F
25. T

JACOBS' GEOMETRY

A Respected Standard for Teaching Geometry

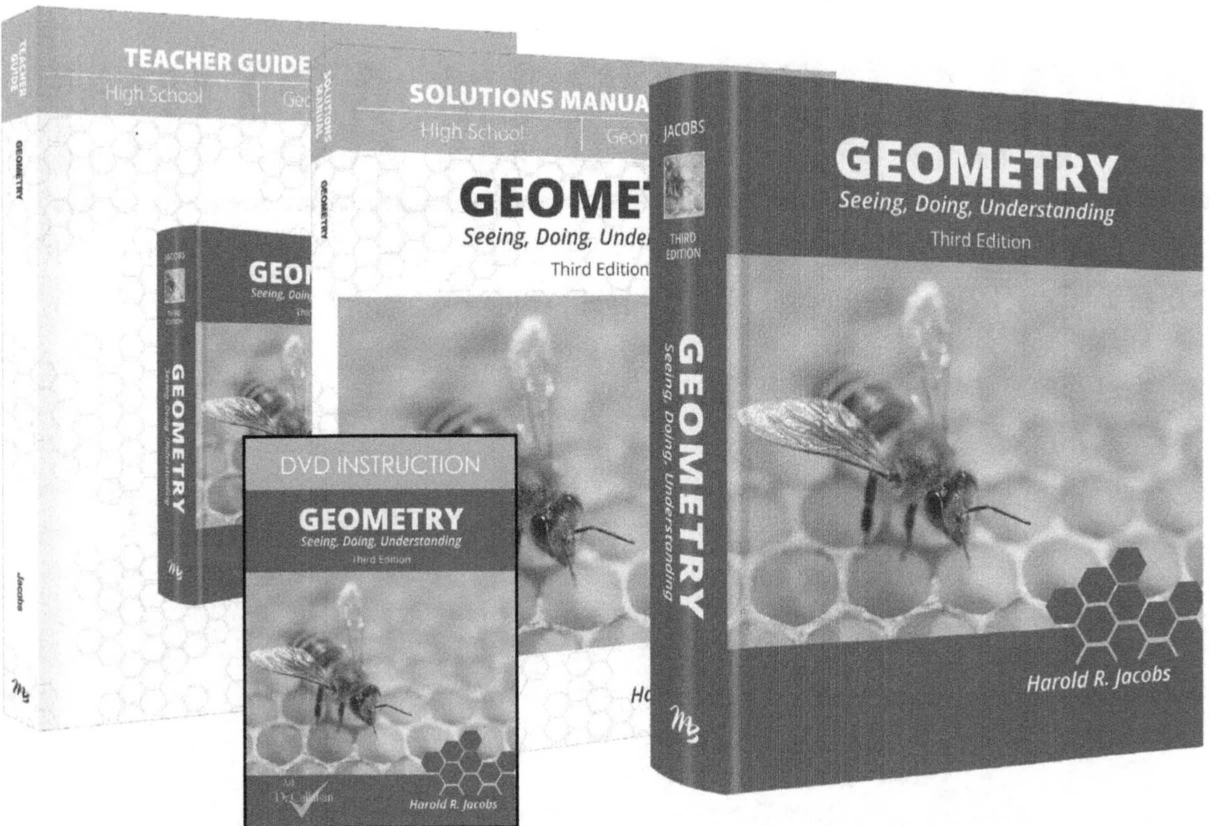

Harold Jacobs' *Geometry* has been an authoritative standard for years, with nearly one million students having learned geometry principles through the text. Now revised with a daily schedule, the text is adaptable for either classroom or homeschool use. With the use of innovative discussions, cartoons, anecdotes, and vivid exercises, students will not only learn but will also find their interest growing with each lesson. The full-color student book focuses on guided discovery to help students develop geometric awareness. Geometry is all around us. Prepare to understand its dynamic influence so much better!

Jacobs' Geometry	978-1-68344-020-8
Solutions Manual	978-1-68344-021-5
Teacher Guide	978-1-68344-022-2
3-BOOK SET	**978-1-68344-036-9**
Geometry DVD	713438-10236-8
3-BOOK / 1-DVD SET	**978-1-68344-037-6**

AVAILABLE AT
MASTERBOOKS.COM 800.999.3777
& OTHER PLACES WHERE FINE BOOKS ARE SOLD.

APOLOGETICS IN ACTION

DISCOVER HOW THE BIBLE PROVES ITSELF, AND THE INSIGHT YOU NEED TO STRENGTHEN YOUR FAITH AND DEFEND GOD'S WORD

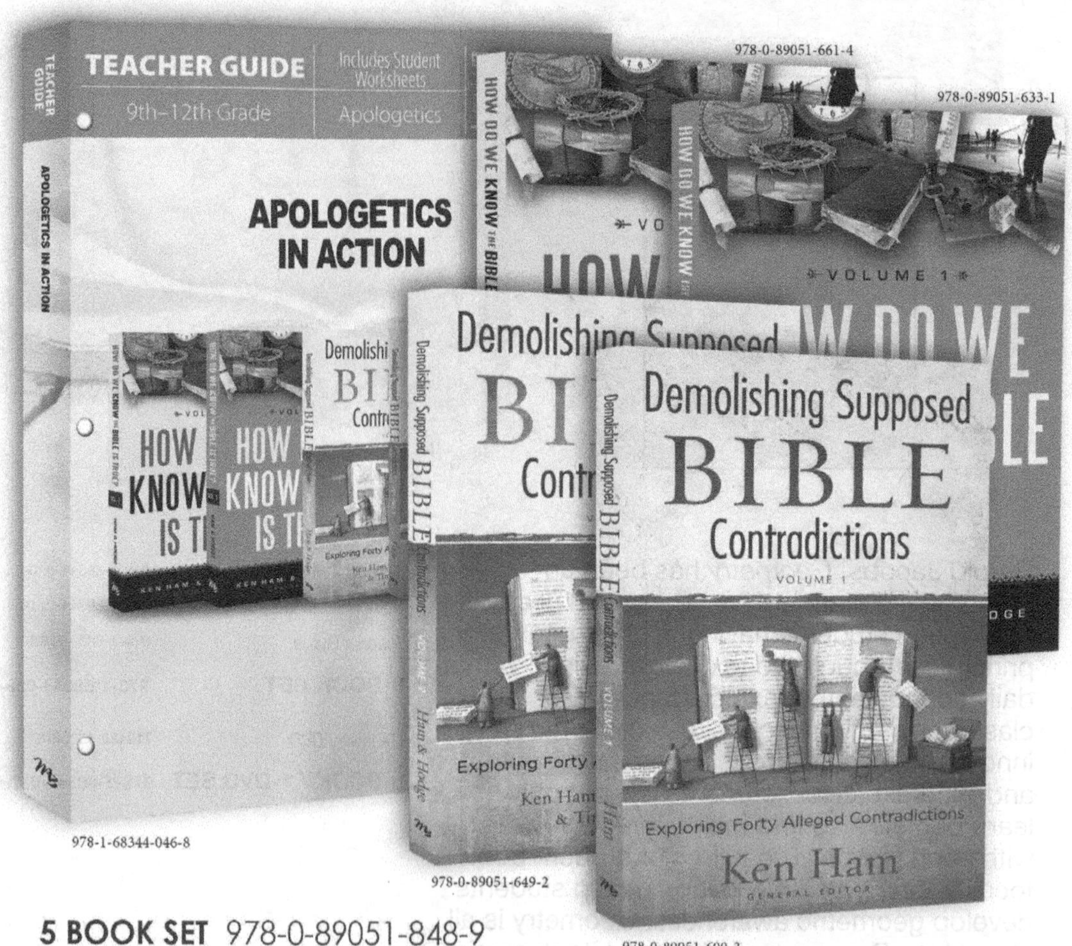

5 BOOK SET 978-0-89051-848-9

AVAILABLE AT
MASTERBOOKS.COM & OTHER PLACES WHERE FINE BOOKS ARE SOLD.

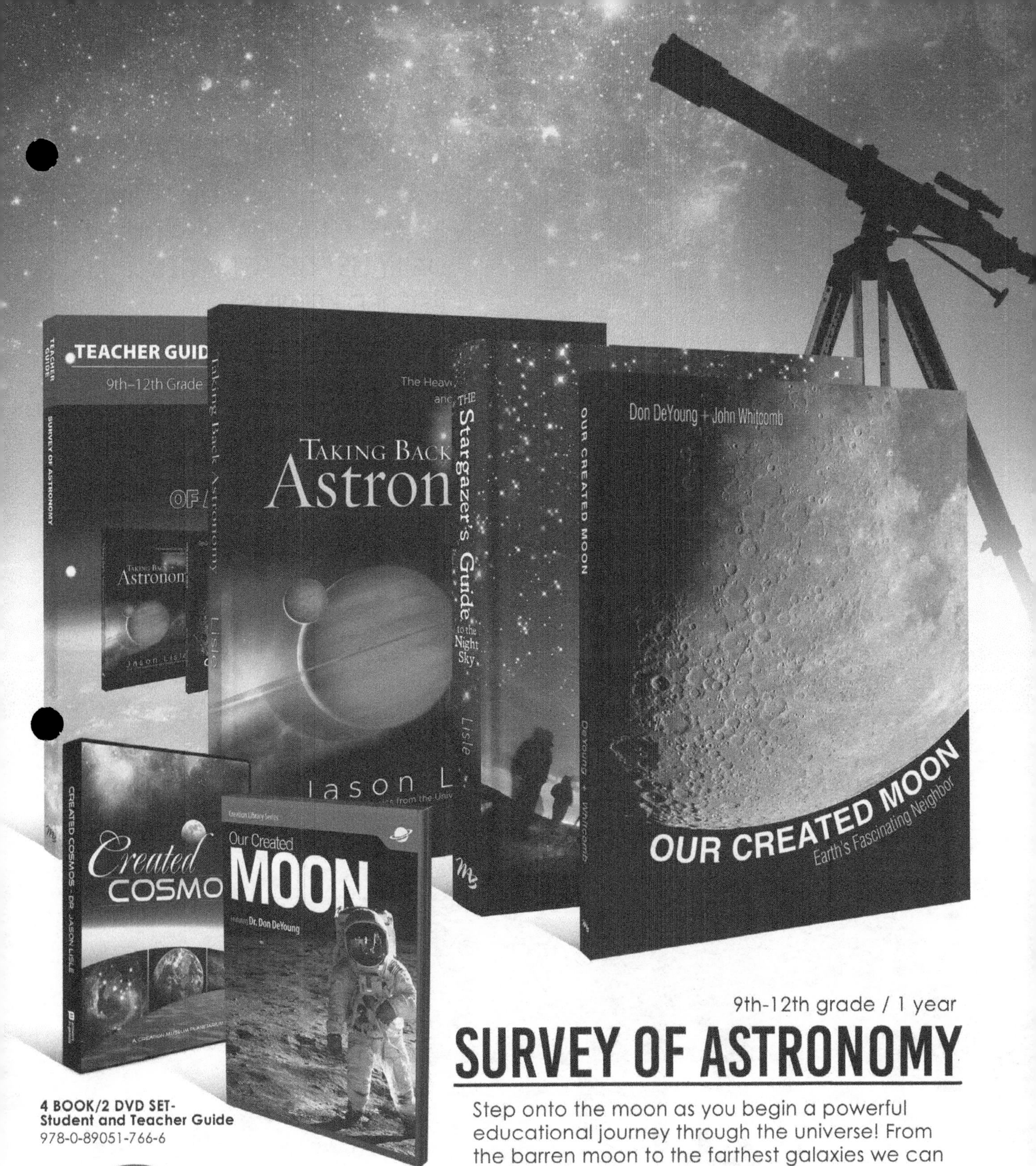

4 BOOK/2 DVD SET-
Student and Teacher Guide
978-0-89051-766-6

9th-12th grade / 1 year

SURVEY OF ASTRONOMY

Step onto the moon as you begin a powerful educational journey through the universe! From the barren moon to the farthest galaxies we can see, you will learn about the facts and wonders of this marvel of creation. Teams solid science with a biblical perspective to answer important questions about the stars, planets, and the place of Earth in this vast expanse!

AVAILABLE AT MASTERBOOKS.COM — Where Faith Grows! — & OTHER PLACES WHERE FINE BOOKS ARE SOLD.

Daily Lesson Plans

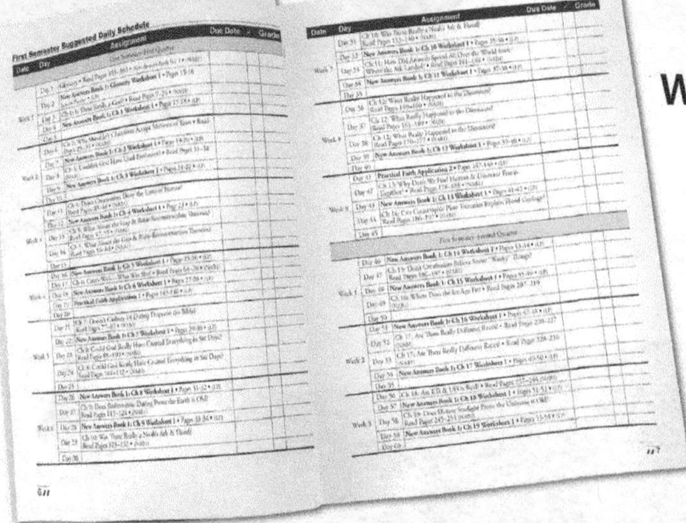
First Semester Suggested Daily Schedule

WE'VE DONE THE WORK FOR YOU!

PERFORATED & 3-HOLE PUNCHED
FLEXIBLE 180-DAY SCHEDULE
DAILY LIST OF ACTIVITIES
RECORD KEEPING

"THE TEACHER GUIDE MAKES THINGS SO MUCH EASIER AND TAKES THE GUESS WORK OUT OF IT FOR ME."

HOMESCHOOL

Master Books® Homeschool Curriculum

Faith-Building Books & Resources
Parent-Friendly Lesson Plans
Biblically-Based Worldview
Affordably Priced

Master Books® is the leading publisher of books and resources based upon a Biblical worldview that points to God as our Creator.

Now the books you love, from the authors you trust like Ken Ham, Michael Farris, Tommy Mitchell, and many more are available as a homeschool curriculum.

MASTERBOOKS.COM
Where Faith Grows!